EMDR
for Anxiety

**Powerful Self-Guided Tools for Overcoming
Panic, Fear, Stress, and Worry**

ESTHER GOLDSTEIN, LCSW

New Harbinger Publications, Inc.

Publisher's Note

NEW HARBINGER PUBLICATIONS is a registered
trademark of New Harbinger Publications, Inc.

New Harbinger Publications is an employee-owned company.

Copyright © 2026 by Esther Goldstein
       New Harbinger Publications, Inc.
       5720 Shattuck Avenue
       Oakland, CA 94609
       www.newharbinger.com

All Rights Reserved

Cover design by Amy Shoup

Acquired by Wendy Milstine and Jed Bickman

Edited by Jenifer Holder

Library of Congress Cataloging-in-Publication Data on file

Printed in the United States of America

28   27   26

10   9   8   7   6   5   4   3   2   1   First Printing

To the seekers, the feelers, the brave—
those who whisper softly,
"There must be more than this ache,"
and step forward with quiet hope.
To the ones who keep going, even when it's hard.
Who are learning to meet themselves with gentleness,
one breath, one moment at a time.
To the healers who hold pain with open hands,
offering their presence as a steady light—
walking alongside others on the path to wholeness and joy.
Whether you are walking through your own healing
or holding space for someone else's—
may these pages meet you where you are.
May they bring relief, reflection, and the reminder
that healing is not only possible—it's already beginning.

Contents

Part Four: Tools for Ongoing Resilience

Anxiety Is a Disconnecting Force, But You Are Not Alone

Do you know the feeling of being in a room surrounded by people, but you are swirling in anxiety and feel so far away from them? Anxiety has a way of spinning us into another universe where we feel alone, disconnected from ourselves and others. Because you're human, loneliness is one of the worst feelings possible. The thing is, you're not alone in this experience. All of us experience anxiety—some more severely, some less so—but it is a universal experience. The good news and bad news is this: you're just like all of us. You picked this book up because you're seeking relief from common experiences like these:

- Sitting at a party where social anxiety has taken hold, so you sit on the sidelines when you desperately want to connect with others.

- Gasping as you breathe heavily, trying to ride out a panic attack, feeling terrified of the intensity.

- Hiding away from your partner and kids, thinking, *I just don't feel right, this nagging irritability is eating at me.*

- Thinking about your future with a pit in your stomach because you're scared of what's to come.

- Navigating strong emotions from the past that spring up in your memory.

You're seeking a life jacket to survive some, or all, of this. Whatever you may be experiencing, please know you are not crazy, you're not alone in this experience—and most importantly—you do not need to suffer this way for the rest of your life. Picking this book up is a step in the right direction. Anxiety gets in the way of connection. As you reduce and resolve your anxiety, you'll have more freedom to engage with yourself and others.

Now, try something with me. Close your eyes for a few seconds and think about the word "anxiety." What happens? Does your...

- body tense up?

- shoulders rise toward your ears?

- stomach get rumbly or tight?

- heart start racing?

- thoughts recall an upsetting memory?

- imagination produce a fearful scenario?

If any of these reactions resonate, it makes sense. Words send our minds and bodies messages. I like to think of experiencing anxiety as *energy on overdrive*. The human experience requires energy. Energy feeds us and fires us up. It's what pushes us to love, dream, and navigate possibilities in life. At the same time, if our energy is constantly in "overdrive," like a car pushing eighty miles per hour when driving down a neighborhood block, our minds and bodies become exhausted, and our resources are depleted.

Anxiety itself is not the problem. When you came into the world, you came with anxiety. Anxiety is essentially your buddy, who needs to be understood and then tended—all your life. There will be times when anxiety ramps up and gets loud. And also times when it will remain at bay, calm and quiet. You may feel like you want to disown anxiety, throw it away, or run from it. But it will return in some shape or form, so instead of shoving it away, you can find ways to work with it. Buddies for life.

The problem isn't anxiety; it's ignoring it. When the "alarm of anxiety" goes off, you likely unconsciously press the snooze button, or try very hard to shut it off altogether. Ultimately these go-to methods are attempts to avoid feeling the anxiety. Though helpful short-term, they can cause your internal alarm to misfire. This faulty alarm system can cause trouble, like an inability to concentrate at work, sleep issues, and physical ailments that can include stomachaches, migraines, and back pain.

In this book, you are going to learn how to unpack what is actually going on when you experience anxiety, beneath the surface. Then, you will explore befriending the parts of you that get anxious. With these tools, anxiety can actually become a welcome part of your human experience. Yes, anxiety can help you recognize potential dangers. And it can also have important things to tell you. If you listen to your anxiety, it often has some wisdom to offer about an unmet need, fear, or hope that needs your attention.

You can cultivate the right mindset to digest and process what the anxiety is communicating. You may even learn to appreciate your anxious parts and the important messages they try to share with you. With a little support and plenty of effort, you can learn to befriend your anxiety, recognize its voice, and channel its energy in productive ways. Then, instead of feeling the need to run away or shush the inner noise, you'll have more emotional energy and mental capacity to connect with loved ones, be creative, and focus on what matters most to you.

I'm excited to share that anxiety doesn't have to hold you back or hinder your quality of life. I'm a human who knows anxiety all too well. I've also been treating clients with anxiety for close to fifteen years in my therapy practice, and supervising clinicians in my group practice. In a training program I run, I teach therapists how to help their clients with anxiety. Anxiety and stress affect so many of us. By opening this book, you've already achieved a remarkable feat. You've found the courage to seek new tools and insights that can help you navigate anxiety more effectively. I'm honored to be your guide on this journey of learning to use these powerful techniques from eye movement desensitization and reprocessing (EMDR).

Leading Yourself Wisely Through the EMDR Journey

EMDR is a transformative therapy that helps us get through stuck points and superficial Band-Aid healing. It can quickly and significantly help us reach a place of deep healing. Using this tool, you will no longer feel lost in the abyss of your anxiety. With EMDR-style activities, you can repair your body's internal alarm system and begin training your body to respond differently to anxiety. EMDR opens up a world of possibilities for healing and growth.

With this book, EMDR techniques are made accessible to you, regardless of socioeconomic status, time availability, background, or education level. Historically, EMDR required a therapist and multiple sessions to orchestrate it. This unfortunately made an effective and transformative technique inaccessible to a lot of people. I want to empower people to take charge of their anxiety, on their own, using an adaptation of the classic EMDR techniques without the therapist.

I do want to say this: It's true that EMDR is a therapeutic technique best practiced with a trained professional. A therapist is absolutely crucial when dealing with trauma. A therapist can be especially helpful in the beginning of any wellness journey and also to get through bumps along the way. But understanding that not everyone has access to such a resource, I've adapted EMDR-style techniques in this book, so anyone can benefit from its transformative power independently. If you do have the means, I encourage you to get started with a therapy professional and then use this book as supplementary material.

During this journey, we'll look at some past memories together. If you have a history of trauma, exploring these memories can be painful. I can't guide you through those deeper and darker places with just a book. If you start to feel lost in the emotions of your memories, reach out for support from a trauma specialist. A well-trained professional is like your human lifeline or a flashlight in the darkness. Specialists in your area can be found on the EMDR website https://www.emdria.org/find-an-emdr-therapist/.

In this book, I can offer many methods to access your own wisdom and ability to hold your emotions with compassion, clarity, and strength.

When you are your own best resource for handling anxiety, a life of possibility opens up. In other words, I aim to guide you so that by the end of this book, you can guide yourself. That is my hope for you.

How to Use This Book

The journey through anxiety with EMDR is not linear. Like so much in life, both anxiety and access to wise parts of ourselves are experiences that come and go. I encourage you to read through this book once, in a linear way, but after that you're in control of this adventure. You can refer back to any section, decide where to go, how much time to dedicate, and who else you may need to bring along for the trek. For a cross-country drive, you would prepare a roadmap and decide where you'll visit in advance, to set goals for yourself. Think of the journey through this book similarly, where the way might be clear but the actual experience you have depends on so many varying conditions.

I encourage you to document your experiences on this journey. If you enjoy creativity, start a special scrapbook or art journal dedicated to your healing process. You can include the most meaningful activities and reflections as we progress. It will be a beautiful keepsake of your growth and transformation. If artsy stuff intimidates you, or you enjoy organization, dedicate a journal, binder, or notebook to this journey. Keep it handy so you can jot down ideas and notes, and also track your progress.

You don't have to be perfect at this process; in fact I encourage you to be willing to do it imperfectly. You can take all the time you need to improve your relationship with anxiety. The fastest way to see results is to go slow. I like to think of it as lifting weights at the gym. Push too hard and you risk "injury," push too little and nothing is gained. If anything in this book triggers you, it's *essential* to listen to your inner alarm bells, put the book down, and seek the guidance of an EMDR-trained trauma specialist before proceeding. Your well-being is my number-one priority. Please challenge yourself in a very balanced and conscious way.

Throughout the book, you'll find journal prompts and activities to further enhance your exploration. You can also access additional resources to download at http://www.integrativepsych.co/emdrfor anxiety. Feel free to engage all these prompts and try out each of the additional activities, as much as you can. Remember, this is your journey, and you have the power to make it as meaningful and impactful as possible. I invite you to join me and self-lead your way to living your best life.

Part One

Anxiety in Your Body, Mind, and World

Chapter 1

Your Internal Alarm Bells

Anxiety is a normal response when we face stress or any sort of challenging situation. Our intuitive bodies are brilliantly designed to keep us safe. We each have an internal alarm system that adapts and evolves with us as we grow and develop. When our body senses danger, alarm bells make all sorts of noise to get our attention. Here's the thing, though. When our internal alarm goes off, our body has no idea if the threat is real or not. Often our internal alarm gets tripped, not by what's happening in the moment, but by a memory imprint. Based on past "danger" experiences or memories stored on our DNA's "hard drive," the brain makes a quick, impulsive calculation and sends messages that put the body into super-hyperdrive protection mode. When that happens, all nonessential parts of our nervous system, like parts of our brain in charge of logic and reasoning, shut down so we can focus on dealing with the threat at hand.

Sometimes, our body can be a bit too cautious. It may sound the loudest alarms—usually reserved for world catastrophes or life-threatening situations—even when there's no immediate or serious danger. When this happens regularly, the constantly activated alarm puts a lot of stress on our nervous system, just as running a marathon all day, every day, without a break would put tremendous strain on our joints and muscles. Over time, the wear and tear can lead to problems like chronic fatigue, back pain, migraines, burnout, emotional dysregulation, anxiety, depression and all sorts of illnesses. As you read this book, you are going to learn to balance your life and help your nervous system become better at identifying and regulating false alarms.

This book is specifically about helping with anxiety, but there is a very close relationship between anxiety and trauma. They affect our bodies and minds almost identically. Our nervous system can become extra sensitive from a single major traumatic event, living in a toxic environment with ongoing microtraumas that you may not even realize are traumas, and chronic unchecked anxiety. Big traumas are much more overt, with better understood repercussions. But ongoing anxiety and chronic stress are like having an alarm hidden somewhere that's low on battery power. You can't find the alarm, so you're living with the irritating beeping noise, adapting until it either gets worse to the point that you can no longer ignore it or the batteries wear out completely. This is what happens with high-functioning anxiety. You adapt and keep going until you just can't anymore. The techniques and tools therapists use to treat trauma provide the same support for chronic anxiety. Similar methods can help you locate those hidden alarms and recharge, or change, the batteries so they're no longer blaring all the time.

Anxiety Is a Response to Stress

Like anxiety, stress is a natural part of our journey through life, something that most people encounter on a daily basis. It's our body's response to anything that requires our attention or action. Our nervous system recognizes a change and says, "Hey, something important is happening here, pay attention!" Stress isn't good or bad. You might be surprised to hear that in small doses, stress can actually be helpful. Similar to weight training, our bodies are designed to handle—and even get stronger—with short bursts of stress. But not the long-lasting kind.

In a society that values constant work and busyness, chronic stress can be par for the course. There's no official diagnosis for it, but the common symptoms of chronic stress can mimic other mental and physical illnesses. Not only that, chronic stress can also increase our risk of developing illnesses, especially if we have a genetic predisposition to certain conditions.

The feeling of chronic stress can be like wearing a ten-pound bag of flour on your back. Like strength training, that extra weight can help in short spurts. But carry it too long and you will cause damage. Many of us inherit these "big bags of flour," never learning that we can (and should) take them off our shoulders and rest. We learn to shame our-selves and we learn to cope, which just becomes new maladaptive responses to stress. If you grew up in an environment where stress is seen as a status symbol, you might learn to ignore your own intuition and push too hard. Thankfully it's still possible to learn to lessen the load so you can channel the stress to your benefit instead of letting it break you.

Our bodies are equipped with an incredible system to protect us from stress. When we face challenges, big or small, our bodies kick into action, treating those challenges as threats. Your *stress response* is an inborn defense mechanism that keeps you safe. It works like this:

- At the heart of this defense system is a part of your brain called the *hypothalamus*. It acts as the commander, sound-ing alarm bells when it senses danger. It sends nerve signals and releases special hormones that tell your body, "Hey, we're in a tough situation here, so let's gear up for a battle!"

- One of the hormones it releases is *adrenaline*, which boosts your heart rate, increases blood pressure, and gives you a surge of energy. When stress levels increase, some people thrive and get things done more efficiently. Others quickly burn through the extra energy and end up shutting down completely.

- Another important hormone is *cortisol*, known as the "stress hormone." It serves as a sort of team manager, coor-dinating your body's response. Cortisol tells your body to gather all the energy it can find, stored in different parts of the body that are not needed during a crisis. This increases the sugar levels in your bloodstream, sending fuel to the parts of your brains that you need in crisis, as well as only the most important organs, tissue, and muscles (as a triage situation). Energy from the less essential organs is used sort of like a backup generator, to make sure the most impor-tant functions keep running smoothly during this crisis. Unfortunately included in those parts that get shut down is the part of the brain in charge of executive functions like self-regulation, reason, and logic. That's why when stressed, we can be easily triggered and react impulsively, in ways we later feel embarrassed about.

This is what is known as an *autonomic response* to stress. Anxiety is one of many stress responses. It's a little messenger in our mind that has the ability to serve as an early warning system, if we learn to hear it early enough. When anxiety is functioning well, it's like having helpful first-responders to protect us from danger. Anxiety signals, "Hey, something important is about to happen. Stay on your toes!" However, when maladaptive anxiety takes over, instead of being helpful, it can cause us bigger problems. Here's how anxiety affected Kevin.

When Kevin walks into my office, he seems to have it all together. He is wearing a tailored suit with his initials monogrammed on the cuffs. His cologne quickly fills the room with a rustic, woody scent. His body language exudes strength. As he passes the mirror hanging on the wall, he smiles at himself and adjusts his tie. I ask Kevin what brought him to my office.

Still grinning, he responds, "I'm nervous all the time. My life seems okay, but inside I'm panicking as if there's some impending doom! I'm becoming exhausted by it."

"Tell me about what it feels like inside, with the nervous feeling."

He exhales. "Esther, it's so draining. And confusing. I work hard at making myself look calm and composed because I need to give my family and colleagues a sense of safety. But inside, I feel like a terrified little kid, anxious about everything. I worry about my success, my kid's safety, not being enough for my partner so that she will leave me one day…." The list goes on. As he talks about his anxiety, and the fears, his body tenses and his speech speeds up. He grows animated.

"Sometimes my worry prevents me from doing things that would make my life richer. I am afraid to feel too happy because it could end at any moment. I don't want to jinx things." A streak of worry crosses his face. Almost terror. It's like he is terrified of letting go and trusting, because his life may fall apart under his feet. He's

seeking safety but he doesn't feel safe internally. I listen as he goes on.

"I didn't even realize that I was anxious about these things until I started getting migraines, low back pain, and irritable bowel syndrome. My doctor couldn't find any physical reason why I have been experiencing this torture." Kevin's doctor sensed that there was underlying anxiety behind the physical symptoms, so he had recommended that Kevin come learn some EMDR skills.

Kevin's worries were exhausting to hold. He seemed to have a beautiful life yet he couldn't focus on it. Brené Brown calls this "foreboding joy." It happens when we're too anxious to feel joy, in case it goes away. So we hold back from engaging fully in our lives. Maybe you are also afraid that you will ruin the good things you have, so you don't want to get too used to it. Or you fear something bad will inevitably happen and you will not be equipped to handle it. Perhaps you worry that if anyone sees how vulnerable and weak you really are, you won't be respected anymore. But it's so lonely to have an outside persona that's so different from all the thoughts inside.

Now, if you are like Kevin—an organized, outgoing, seemingly successful person, who others think is conquering the world—you may be experiencing *high-functioning anxiety* (HFA). You feel exhausted on the inside, but on the outside you have everything under control—like a superhero. HFA superheroes are usually very productive. And at the same time, you may not know how or when to rest, replenish, ask for help, or connect with others.

While being a superhero has perks, there is always a cost to pay or a kryptonite lurking close by. The cost is that your internal alarm is always on high alert, getting very little down time. This causes lots of wear and tear on the nervous system that people on the outside don't see. You may not even realize the price you're paying until you start getting migraines or chronic pain or start being less efficient.

The Toll Anxiety Takes

Any type of chronic stress or anxiety can take a toll on our bodies and minds if we don't learn a sense of balance. Anxiety can go from being highly functional to a more severe challenge that requires intervention. *Anxiety disorders* can happen for different reasons. Sometimes, it's because of our genetics. Other times, it's because we've constantly ignored our alarms or avoided certain situations that make us anxious instead of finding healthier ways to cope.

One common anxiety disorder is called *generalized anxiety disorder (GAD)*. It feels like having a nonstop worry machine in your brain. The worrying becomes so overwhelming that it starts to interfere with daily life. Even simple things like taking showers, hanging out with friends, or attending appointments can become overwhelming. It can cause headaches, trouble sleeping, exhaustion, and difficulty focusing. If you try some self-help strategies from this book and you're still struggling with your day-to-day life, it's time to reach out to a professional.

There are many different types of anxiety disorders, each with unique features. While we won't explore details of the various disorders in this book, it's important to recognize when anxiety is affecting your ability to enjoy life and connect with others. Seeking help is a courageous step toward finding the support you need to live your best life. This book is here to help you with "garden variety" anxiety symptoms. But if you are concerned you may have a disorder, it's important to seek professional help. This book can definitely be used alongside clinical help, but it's not a quick fix for a clinical disorder requiring clinical interventions.

The Link Between Trauma and Anxiety

Your anxiety may have some elements of trauma that contribute to your suffering. According to many experts, *trauma* is when our nervous system is exposed to real or perceived threat, and gets overwhelmed by anything that happens too much, too soon, or too fast to handle. It's like playing an advanced level of Tetris and all the pieces just keep coming down so quickly that you have no ability to keep up with moving the pieces around, so you can no longer clear rows. The pieces just pile up and block access to the parts of the board you are trying to reach. Eventually the pile reaches its max and you are stuck.

Trauma and stress often go hand in hand. The terms may be used interchangeably because they both involve our nervous system feeling overwhelmed. Trauma can happen when something external, like an event or experience, shakes us to our core, overwhelming our nervous system and changing the way we process and remember things. Our mind-body connection is thrown out of sync.

A traumatic event disrupts our sense of safety, control, and overall well-being. A traumatic event affects each of us differently. What might be traumatic for one person may not impact another. Additionally, when we encounter a traumatic event, it may not necessarily cause trauma to our nervous system. A physical, blunt-force trauma like a concussion may be a straightforward physical injury to overcome with no residual impact to the nervous system or psyche. It will all depend on a combination of factors. Some of us can process and make sense of our experiences quicker and more effectively than others.

When we think of the word trauma, we often picture big, epic events like a world war, a massive tsunami, or a meteor crashing down and destroying a city. These are called *big T traumas*. They're caused by experiencing major events that everyone can recognize as traumatic. It's normal and healthy to get thrown off-kilter when these kinds of events happen. There's another kind of trauma, though, that can be much harder to spot. These are called *small t traumas, complex traumas,* or *cumulative stress*. Small t traumas are like tiny cuts or bruises that don't have a chance to heal before they get hurt again and again. These tiny boo-boos build up in our nervous systems over time, often without us realizing it. They can come from either active or passive things like microaggressions, shame, neglect, bullying, regularly feeling lonely, feeling judged, or not building healthy and strong connections with other people. Each one might not seem like a big deal on its own, but they can cause damage when added up. When these small t traumas pile up, symptoms can be almost identical to big T trauma symptoms, causing struggles throughout our life, affecting us physically and emotionally. Any sort of trauma is the main contributor to symptoms of anxiety.

Both traumatic events and seemingly benign stressful situations have the power to alert our central nervous system to spring into action. Either one can act like a tripwire that derails us or makes us feel stuck, triggering physical and emotional reactions throughout our body that are called *trauma responses*. Internally, they are pretty much the same as stress responses. There is very little difference between the way our body responds to trauma and stress. The main difference is the degree of intensity, which differs from person to person, largely dependent on whether or not we have developed effective coping skills.

A trauma response can happen even when there is no immediate traumatic incident. For example, if you were in a life-threatening car accident, years later you may go out for dinner and hear a loud crashing noise coming from the kitchen. The noise could trigger a trauma response inside you. The response is usually so intense that it can be challenging for you to process and integrate what's happening in your current reality. Your nervous system makes a split-second association that causes your mind to time travel. This can happen even if the original event didn't seem traumatic at the time.

Your unique life circumstances, risk factors, and genetic makeup influence how your nervous system processes and responds to all kinds of experiences. As you'll learn in later chapters, when you start to notice patterns in the types of situations that cause you to react, as well as the types of responses you experience, you can learn to prepare and calm the nervous system down *before* reacting. Or you can help the nervous system recover faster and more efficiently. The self-regulation tools you will learn can help you navigate challenges better and cultivate greater resilience. While this book is not meant to help heal bigger forms of trauma, it can be a great accompaniment to trauma therapy. Your therapist can help you navigate some of the trickier parts of your journey and you can use this book on the side, in between sessions.

The great news is that our body is naturally equipped with the mechanisms to heal and grow from trauma if we tap into those internal resources. We can find ways to process and integrate overwhelming experiences. When we seek support after facing significant trauma and invest time and energy into healing, we can emerge even stronger than before.

Responses to Stress

As psychiatrist Bessel van der Kolk writes, "After trauma, the world is experienced with a different nervous system that has an altered perception of risk and safety" (2015). If a traumatic or stressful situation happens when we are five years old, our responses should be very different from the way we would respond as a twenty-five year old. This is because as we mature, we hopefully have developed newer, more adaptive responses to triggers.

Have you ever been in a fight with someone and acted in a completely childish way in the heat of the moment? Maybe you hit, threw a tantrum, or screamed at the top of your lungs. After calming down, you felt embarrassed because you realized how immature you sounded. That type of immature response is known as *maladaptive*. While it's normal, age-appropriate behavior for a five-year-old child, it's not at twenty-five years old. An *adaptive response* to a fight would include pausing for reflection, taking a time-out to calm down, or communicating calmly.

Many of the symptoms associated with high-functioning anxiety and anxiety disorders were actually normal, adaptive responses at one point in your life. When a situation becomes too much, too intense, or lasts for too long, we tend to revert back to those old, childlike behaviors because a "child part" has been stirred up to the surface. That "child part" became a part of your inner world back when those behaviors were actually adaptive. Now that we understand the behaviors are clearly maladaptive, we can help that "child part" feel seen and heard. In the coming chapters, you will learn to identify your "anxious parts" and teach them newer, more adaptive ways to respond to similar stressful situations. For now, we'll explore the first thing you can do to contain your feelings of overwhelm in the heat of the moment.

Create Emotional Space Through Containment

Sometimes intense reactions to triggers can catch us by surprise, like a sudden flash flood during an unexpected storm. They can happen when we least expect them. That's why it's important to learn some basic containment skills right from the start. This will help you clear away the debris of initial dysregulation so you can tap into your adaptive responses as soon as possible.

Containment exercises are not meant to make your distressing thoughts, feelings, sensations, or memories disappear. No, no! You can use containment to carefully "shelf" gnawing thoughts, filing them in a safe place. You can deal with them later, from a calmer, more level-headed place, at a more opportune time. When you're ready, you can revisit and process each stressor individually, one by one, step by step.

Exercise: Your Container

Picture a special container sitting right in front of you. It could be a mason jar, a box, a folder, a locker, or anything you can put things into. If you're feeling extra creative, you can draw a picture of it in your journal or actually get a physical jar or box. There is also a free download at http://www.integrativepsych.co/emdr foranxiety called Containment Primer that you can print and use.

Imagine that this container is no ordinary object—it has magical powers! Notice the details of your container. What color is it? Is it made of glass, wood, or something else? Does it feel warm or cool to the touch? Are there any interesting decorations on it? Let your imagination, or your artistic talents, run wild!

Now that you have the most fantastic container, let's fill it up with all the things that are troubling you. It could be distressing thoughts, memories, body sensations, aches and pains, or emotions. If you have a physical container or a picture of one, you can write or draw each item on small pieces of paper and put them inside. If you're visualizing, imagine placing them in your container, one by one.

Once you've filled your container, it's time to seal it up. Whether with a physical lid or an imaginary one, visualize that you are closing the lid up tight.

Take a moment to appreciate the magic of containment. All those stray thoughts and worries are now safely stored away. You don't have to worry about forgetting or losing any of it—everything is in there, waiting for you to deal with them, one by one, when you're ready.

With your thoughts contained, notice how clear your mind feels. Instead of ruminating on stray intrusive thoughts, you're now free to focus on thoughts you choose to focus on. You can focus on one thing at a time, making calm and rational choices about what you want to address and how. Remember, you're not avoiding these stressors and buzzing thoughts forever. You're simply shelving them for later, when you're prepared to face them at your choosing, from a calm and grounded place. Once you do this, you may find that you can tolerate more without feeling so overwhelmed.

Picture this: you are on a hike, enjoying the great outdoors, when you spot the first signs of a thunderstorm brewing above. But wait! You see a cozy cave nearby that you can quickly climb into. Inside the cave, you are safe and dry, watching the storm unfold from a distance. You can observe the pouring rain and roaring thunder without getting swept away by the currents. That's exactly what containment is all about. It's finding a safe space where you can engage your feelings without getting overwhelmed by them. In the next chapter, we'll dive further into more ways you can do this.

Chapter 2

Tolerance of Emotional Extremes

Even with your anxious thoughts and emotions contained, you can expect emotions to ebb and flow—it's part of being human. But how much ebb and flow can you tolerate? What emotional extremes trigger maladaptive responses and what tools help you maintain adaptive responses? These questions are a part of getting to know your own tolerance of emotional extremes. Even if you become a superstar at knowing your limits and living within your zone, you will still experience ups and downs and challenges beyond your control. The goal is therefore not to avoid potentially painful situations altogether, living in a bubble. Ultimately, you want to learn more adaptive tools and develop more self-awareness so your emotional responses become, as a baseline, less extreme one way or the other (unless you face immediate stress, a crisis, or an emotionally intense experience). This type of resilience will help you become more grounded and balanced—and less anxious—in your daily life. Professor of psychiatry Dan Siegel calls this sweet spot of existence our *window of tolerance* (Siegel 1999). Staying within our window of tolerance is an optimal state of being, where we can function at our best and thrive in daily life. In this mode, our thoughts become clearer, our communication improves, and we can maintain greater inner peace.

The Emotional Pendulum

We can emotionally swing to one extreme or the other, moving outside our window of tolerance and becoming either *hyperaroused* or *hypoaroused* (Ogden et al. 2006). This spectrum varies in degrees from person to person, and ranges from feeling overly intense amounts of excitement (hyperaroused) to feeling catatonically down in the dumps (hypoaroused). These extreme states can hinder our ability to behave, feel, think, and respond in balanced and rational ways.

When we are chronically stressed or have experienced trauma, whether big or small, our tolerance zone will often be narrower. This makes our breaking point a lot quicker and easier to reach. If you live with functional anxiety, you might notice that certain times of the year, specific people, or types of life experiences can affect the bandwidth of your tolerance levels. Through a regular mindful practice of staying in the zone, you can expand your breadth of tolerance and enjoy more emotional stability. Throughout your journey with this book, you'll learn how to navigate, find balance, and regulate emotional extremes. It all happens in the *autonomic nervous system (ANS)*.

The ANS, also known as "auto-response," "emergency response," or "alarm bells," controls pretty much everything that goes on in the body when we are not consciously making other efforts. We don't often think about how miraculous it is because everything happens behind the scenes in our brain (the subconscious). The ANS does things like circulating our blood, digesting our food, breathing, going to the bathroom, and making our heart beat. As we grow and practice, we can gain more abilities that become automated like walking and riding a bike. This system is made up of different parts, mainly the sympathetic and parasympathetic nervous systems.

- The *parasympathetic* ANS is our healthy working dashboard. It's the sensor for our internal alarm system that can efficiently bring heightened emotional states back to states of calm, balance, and logic without throwing our nervous systems out of whack. It allows for rest, digestion, and homeostasis.

- The *sympathetic* ANS has the primary job of quickly sounding the alarm that triggers the body's fight-or-flight responses. The part of the nervous system in charge of sending out these messages is called the *vagus nerve*. In order to better regulate our auto-responses and help our internal alarm system learn to decipher the accuracy of danger cues more quickly—so we can behave and respond with less impulsivity, more adaptively—we need to build and tone the vagus nerve like a muscle.

Experts in polyvagal theory call this kind of strength training "vagal tone strengthening." This is basically what we will be doing throughout this book. Andrea's story shows why toning our tolerance of emotional experiences is so important.

When I meet with Andrea, she's maxed out, like an energizer bunny with depleted batteries, but she can't stop. Her posture is slouched, her curly hair is unkempt, and tears streak down her cheeks. She fidgets, struggling to find a comfortable position.

When I ask her why she has come to therapy, she admits that she doesn't really know why she is in my office. All she knows is that she has reached a breaking point and can no longer manage her life the way it has been going. I usually get a lot of information during a first intake session, but Andrea's emotional dysregulation makes it challenging for her to communicate effectively with me. I learn a lot about her as I read between the lines.

After a half hour, I begin to understand that like so many of us, she is overloaded with responsibilities she doesn't feel equipped to handle. She has a demanding job, her boss is a workaholic and requires all of her when she is at work. She is a single parent of two active little boys, and while her ex-husband shares responsibilities, he often flakes out at the last minute. Her immediate family are at times supportive, and at other times can be emotionally taxing. Andrea has a large circle of friends and finds ways to keep busy. She shares that she has had an "on and off" boyfriend for over a year. That's about all I get before she starts jumping from topic to topic so quickly that it is hard to follow her train of thought.

I wonder if and when she has time to wind down, not just physically, but mentally as well. She seems to be on perpetual speed mode. Some of her responses seem situational, and some seem reinforced by her choices and behavior. Andrea seems to have a lot on her plate, with inadequate support. She also tends to "keep busy" and I wonder what would happen if she found a way to slow down. She is clearly not yet looking for suggestions, or capable of hearing about changes or possible "solutions." She needs to let it all out before we even get to the nuts and bolts of therapy. Before she leaves, I teach her the containment exercise so she can learn to put away all her buzzing thoughts and gain access to her higher-order thinking.

Once Andrea contained her scattered thoughts, feelings, and emotions, she could gain greater awareness of what was really going on inside. When she is calm and somewhat regulated, she can return to *the zone*—the state that will help her start building up her tolerance of emotional intensities. Like Andrea, you can practice the containment tool from the last chapter to settle your frazzled emotional state when you feel that you are reaching your breaking point. This will be helpful as we begin working with the nervous system to strengthen your own tolerance.

How Anxiety Happens in Your Nervous System

The specific area responsible for sending out the alarm bells we've been talking so much about is the back, or dorsal, side of the vagus nerve. This part of the brain connects to the most important organs and body systems, such as the gut, lungs, and heart. When we perceive danger (whether it's real or not), this *dorsal vagal* alarms the nervous system, like a switch, automatically shutting down anything nonessential and turning on anything that will help us get through an emergency situation. This "off switch" shuts down important (yet nonessential) functions that help us maintain balance and health, like attunement, connection, and logic.

To better understand this, imagine that your life was in real danger. If you're trapped in a burning building, you wouldn't try to be more emotionally intimate with your partner or stay focused on hearing your child tell you about the highlights of his day. You would be in action mode, trying to save lives. In emergencies, the self-preservation tools we have inherited or developed over the years to keep us safe are automatic.

Depending on the circumstance, perceived dangers can trigger either hyperarousal or hypoarousal responses. When the vagus nerve is healthy, your alarm bells will work more efficiently—it won't start blaring during nonemergency situations. It will send you little nudges or gentle reminders to respond to nonemergency situations in healthier, less noisy, less destructive ways. When you learn to work with your vagus nerve, you can manage your nervous system rather than letting it derail you.

When we are triggered, our nervous system goes into overdrive, activating and redistributing all our energy reserves. This is commonly known as the *fight, flight, freeze response*, which is a heightened state of hyperarousal. During this activation mode, we tend to have less control of our actions. We might react without thinking clearly, get angry, or feel flooded by emotions and fear. It's like we're driving a car really fast and can't steer or hit the brakes when we need to. Our muscles tighten, panic attacks might happen, and we can't think logically. But fear not! When our amazing nervous system is healthy, it has a built-in mechanism to bring us back into balance, into the zone of emotional tolerance. One of the goals of this book is to teach you how to tap into that natural ability.

Alternatively, being triggered can throw us into the shutdown mode, or "collapse" response, of hypoarousal. This is when our body responds to triggers in a low-energy, power-saving mode, usually when the situation is way too intense to handle. It's our body's way of saying, "Whoa, this is way too much to handle! Abort!" In this mode, our parasympathetic nervous system takes over and our energy level drops. It's like hitting a pause button. We might start to zone out, feel like we have to go to sleep, or seem like we're moving in slow motion. Some even experience *dissociation*, feeling detached from reality. Other common signs of hypoarousal include feeling down, empty, or numb, like we're in a fog. Our body and mind might really need to take a break from reality, so we enter a state of extreme tiredness. Hypoarousal, when left unsupported, can disrupt sleep, eating, and social patterns, making it challenging to navigate daily life.

In actual threatening situations, these responses are lifesaving! These responses are not bad—they're necessary. To pull ourselves out of extreme states, and back into balance, there are strategies we can use. Some include engaging in activities that bring us joy, connecting with supportive friends, and practicing self-care to recharge our energy level.

Signs That You Need to Tend to Yourself

Imagine that a healthy vagus nerve is the working dashboard in your car. It shows you warning lights and makes sounds to tell you if your gas is low or your oil needs changing. As long as you are on top of regular maintenance, you will be forewarned when your car needs some tending, and you can take care of it before anything shuts down or causes problems. When you ignore a low-gas warning for too long, the car might stop in the middle of the highway on your way home from work. If you keep ignoring maintenance warnings, eventually the warnings themselves become unreliable. This is exactly what happens when you ignore your body's messages. Alternatively, when you proactively maintain and service your car regularly, it will likely have a longer, better functioning lifespan. Similarly, when your vagus nerve is well toned, and you listen to the messages your body sends, all systems are working as they should.

The following exercise offers a way to look at, and repair, a malfunctioning dashboard. Once repaired, it can clearly show you what you need to stay healthy, balanced, and able to calmly, efficiently, knowledgeably deal with life challenges as they come up. You can navigate the twists and turns of your inner world while keeping your emotions in check.

Exercise: Pressing the Gas and Break Pedals

Imagine you're behind the wheel of a powerful car on a busy highway. Just like a skilled driver, you are going to use the gas and brake pedals to stay safely behind or in front of other cars, and peripheral vision to avoid road hazards. The goal is to cruise through twists and turns in the road, without having to accelerate too quickly or slam on the brakes too late. You are finding the sweet spot for your own internal settings. I encourage you to regularly ask yourself the following questions. Checking in like this will eventually feel like second nature.

- How am I feeling right now? Am I revved up or feeling a bit sluggish?

- Are there any situations or tasks that are causing me to speed up or slow down?

- Do I need to hit the brakes, taking a moment to ground myself?

- Are there any intrusive thoughts or emotions I need to contain, shelving them for later? If yes, do the containment exercise.

As you go through your day, identify the moments when you need to use brakes and pedals. Your own personal vagus dashboard can help you stay in the optimal range for your emotional balance. With practice, you can become a skilled driver of your own health and well-being, staying aware of messages from your vagus dashboard—no matter how deeply ingrained your reaction patterns are. Your anxiety self-regulation will improve as your awareness and commitment to self-care improves. You have the power to strengthen, maintain, and repair your inner emotional speedometer. It's not about speed. It's not about the destination. It's about a strong commitment to yourself and your inner world journey.

Chapter 3

Early Relationships Cause Anxiety to Repeat

Do you make the same mistakes, or react in ways you promised yourself you wouldn't, over and over again? Maybe you love spending time with your sister, but every time you do, she says something hurtful and you feel bad about yourself. Your anxiety takes hold. You can't stop ruminating about what she said for days and the thoughts distract you at work. Each time this happens, you tell yourself that it will be different this time. You might repeat unhelpful thoughts, like *It's not you, it's her* or *Don't let her get to you—you're better than that.* You may promise that you won't put yourself in that situation again. You set unrealistic boundaries that you know will backfire, such as shortening the visits. You might even find a way to keep your emotions at bay when you are with her. As a result, you feel like you've mastered this particular challenge. Then…you go to grad school and meet a fun, bubbly friend who you just love hanging out with. Every time you go out with her, you have the best time. But at the end of the night, you can't help but feel a tug of familiarity in your gut. You begin to ruminate again. After you meet up with her, you start feeling awful about yourself. Familiar anxieties surface. At first, you don't make the connection to your relationship with your sister, but somehow this relationship is bringing up all your unhealthy thought patterns and you feel a sense of déjà vu.

Sigmund Freud coined the term "repetition compulsion" to describe when we unconsciously recreate past events or repeat unhealthy relationship patterns, almost like we're stuck in a loop. This example of a dynamic with a hypothetical sister shows the repetition compulsion in action. Let's look at how it can contribute to anxiety.

Following the Well-Worn Path

We are drawn to familiar relationship dynamics. Modern research has shed new light on this phenomenon. Psychology's understanding has evolved and the field now realizes that *it's not just in your head*. Repetition compulsion has been explored in psychological, biological, and neurological ways—and EMDR uses this groundbreaking knowledge to support the healing journey.

Here's an analogy to help you visualize what is going on inside your brain when repetition compulsion happens. Imagine you are hiking in an obscure, lush, beautiful forest. You're heading for a healing hot spring next to a magnificent waterfall. Some take a shorter route, but others just follow the well-trodden path and take the scenic route. The latter path is much simpler because you just follow the same path as many other ongoing visitors. It's virtually impossible to lose your way because there are lots of noticeable markers to let you know that you are on the right track. This is similar to how your autonomic nervous system operates.

But then, there is an intense storm, the path is washed out, and trees fall all along it. Many of the familiar signs have been damaged or destroyed. You don't go back for a few weeks, but then you decide to attempt it. You have more difficulty finding the hot spring. You have to forge a new, round-about path in some places and clean up the old one in other places. It's a lot of work, but in the end it's worth it. You even realize you had been previously taking a longer, less efficient route— just because it was the only path you knew well. Turns out there was a better, quicker way to get to the hot spring with more ease.

This is similar to the way our brain functions. With the way our neural pathways are programmed to work, when we go about our days we can get to our "destinations" with ease, as long as there is nothing complicating the path. Our neural pathways are formed by nature and nurture, which are the "foot traffic" that carve out pathways we tend to take, for better or worse. Even if it's not the best route, it's the route we know—carved for us and by us. It's easy. Our brains function really well when we take the paths we know.

When we are challenged in life or triggered by something, and anxiety flares up, it's like inclement weather uprooting and disrupting our regular pathways—figuratively and neurologically. In response, our brains can learn different reroute options. Some are way more difficult (and dysfunctional) than others. For example, children who grew up with little parental guidance will find the best way they can to survive and it's not always the best way. But sometimes, we decide to work hard to find more functional and logical paths. Usually, something big happens that causes us to find newer and healthier ways because, hey, if it ain't broke don't fix it, right? In the short term, changing our ways seems like a lot of work, but in the long run we end up clearing new pathways that are even more functional and efficient than we imagined possible.

So, when we are disrupted, we can either work to keep clearing up the same paths over and over again. Or we can build new pathways that are much easier and faster to repair after the inevitable storms hit. History may naturally repeat itself, but we can take steps to carve out new paths toward the destiny we choose. How do we do that? First, we can understand that it's all about *connection*.

Early Relationships Train Your Personal Autopilot

Consider how many of the challenges you encounter are connected to healing some kind of early relationship. It could be a relationship with yourself, with someone from your past or present, with a higher power, or even with nature. Life is all about connection, and human connections have the power to create new pathways and strengthen old ones. Alternatively, bad relationships can tear down neural connections and create dysfunctional pathways. Our early connections helped shape our brain as we grew and developed, creating a template for how we will connect in future relationships. These templates influenced how we navigate different areas of our life as well, including self-care, work, and family dynamics. How do those templates come to be?

Our early relationships, known as *attachments,* carve out and shape these pathways. They leave imprints on our brain, shaping beliefs about ourselves, others, and the world. These relationships impact how we think, carry ourselves, make decisions, and even socialize. When a mommy gazes lovingly into her baby's eyes, a healthy pathway is created. When a daddy lets his toddler explore the playground while standing right near her, paying close attention to her safety, giving just enough space for her to feel independent, another healthy neural connection is formed. Unhealthy networks can also be formed when basic needs are not met.

Early relationships play a crucial role in structuring our brains. By the time we reach twelve to eighteen months of age, our neural circuitry is mostly "wired" for life (until we learn to grow and adapt). Most memories formed during our formative years operate outside our awareness and are known as *implicit memories.* They give us a template for how to live and function, especially when we're not making conscious decisions when we are tired, stressed, or scared. Our autopilot system kicks in when we need it. This system isn't only activated during a crisis, it also applies to other well-practiced activities like driving to a familiar place without thinking about the directions or playing a musical instrument without thinking about the notes. The more we repeat these activities, the stronger our autopilot neural networks become in that area—just like the well-trodden footpath in the forest.

Unconscious attachment patterns greatly influence how we relate to ourselves (our self-concepts), our perceptions of others, and our interactions with them. When these patterns become maladaptive or overly rigid, life can become challenging to navigate. But the human brain is brilliantly adaptable. As we engage in healing work, we have the power to create new neural circuitry. We can repair the attachment relationships within us, regardless of whether the actual relationship of origin is repairable or not.

Understanding the link between past relationships and current experiences is crucial for understanding the EMDR-based solutions we'll explore in upcoming chapters. So, if it feels like we're jumping around a bit, trust that everything will come together.

The Influence of Your Family of Origin

When I use the phrase *family of origin,* I am referring to primary and secondary caregivers as well as people we spent a majority of our time with during our formative years. We all carry some sort of baggage from our family of origin without realizing it. It's like we have invisible backpacks filled with "stuff" passed down through our genes and it fills more and more throughout our early years. The contents and their "weight" influence what triggers us during interactions with others later on. Our parents and caregivers, whether we like it or not, had a big influence on how we grew emotionally and physically. The emotional energy from our family of origin seeped into us just by being around them (Brown 2006). Even before we were aware of it, these relationships shaped our view of the world, ourselves, and how we would one day connect with others (Peyton 2017).

During those formative years, our family shows us what's good and bad, scary and safe, important and worthless. That's not to say negative traits will always breed negative traits. Sometimes a caregivers' potentially damaging actions influence us to do the opposite of what they did. Nonetheless, our actions are still a result of this connection, for better or for worse. Their influences guide us, whether we actively choose to go in a different direction or soak it all up like a sponge.

Beyond our family, significant events and relationships with best friends, teachers, and other memorable people also play a role in who we have become. They contribute to the formation of our inner world, which can feel like a microcosm of the outer world around us. We develop different parts of our personalities based on what happened to us and how we learn to cope during those crucial years. Here's how Kevin described his experience of this.

> Growing up, my family never had enough money, enough time, or enough piety. My parents both had decent jobs and were respected members of our community, but I remember that there was always worry. I vividly recall sitting at the kitchen table with my parents. They were going on and on, worrying about paying for my bar mitzvah. They said they were going to either take out a new mortgage or make some other financially debilitating decision that I can't remember. I just remember seeing their creased brows, feeling the heaviness that engulfed them, and witnessing sadness in their eyes. I felt awful. I wanted my celebration to bring joy, not pain and despair.

Then and there, I decided that I would own their burdens and fix their problems. I could take on odd jobs to contribute to the family income. Most of my friends were from wealthy families and none of them worked. I was pretty young at the time—twelve, to be exact. I started a business mowing lawns in the summer and shoveling snow in the winter. One of my parent's friends gave me a weekend job stocking shelves at their department store. My grades started to suffer, so I had to work harder to be successful at my jobs and at school. I was working every waking hour to make life easier for my family.

One day, from the other room, I overheard my parents still worrying about money. My dad seemed to be making fun of the fact that I believed all my hard work was going to help. I felt broken and insulted. My mother commented that "it's not enough" and said she was upset that my grades were down. That's what I heard. Who knows what they actually said. But I felt like a failure, even though I was working my butt off. All I heard was that I was never going to be enough. I got sick with stomach pains and migraines, and the doctors could not figure out why. I was not excited about my bar mitzvah, even though it was a beautiful occasion. I had started to believe that nothing that causes that much stress could make me happy.

I learned to suck it up, of course, and always do the right thing. But I find it really hard to enjoy the blessings in life. I wish that I enjoyed my wife and kids more. I wish I enjoyed my financial success more.

We often pick up messages like "I'm never enough" from those closest to us, even though they are not consciously sharing that message. It sounds like Kevin's parents were generally devoted and loving. They didn't know Kevin was listening to their conversation. If they knew how much it shaped Kevin's perception of himself, they would have felt awful. Unfortunately, once a self-perception becomes ingrained, even when circumstances change, a "part" of us is formed. That part's voice remains in our unconscious memories until we learn to engage it and heal it. It will keep telling us this message in different ways throughout our lives, even though we might know cognitively that its messages are untrue.

Cognitively, you can try to coach yourself through hurtful messaging. But inevitably, certain events or people will trigger a visceral reaction that reminds you of that deeply buried youthful "part" and the painfully learned message. Even if you tell yourself that the message and feelings are untrue, this part will still carry the old, harmful self-perception. That is, until this part feels seen, heard, and validated. Kevin's ongoing migraines and stomach pains were telling him that there is a little boy inside, still feeling overwhelmed by never being enough. You will soon learn how to identify and work with your parts and their messages.

Your Capacity to Stop Repeating History

Our perceptions begin to form even before we are born, in utero, while our nervous systems are developing (Clift-Matthews 2010). We are conditioned to see the world, ourselves, and the people around us in ways that become embedded in our nervous system. Nature plays a big role, but nurture also has an impact that depends on what's happening around us. At the same time, incredibly, our body is designed to self-correct. We have an amazing, built-in ability to regulate and heal ourselves, the same way cuts and bruises heal on their own. Generally, our neural pathways can auto-correct because our body naturally strives for balance and harmony, as long as nothing major gets in the way of its development.

As an infant and child, we had a relatively clean slate to form our own perceptions. These perceptions guide most everything we do. When we are given the time and space to make mistakes without shame, and to express healthy curiosity, our perceptions of the world will be healthy and our ability to form relationships will stay strong. Unfortunately, outside damaging influences can prevent the natural growth process. For example, if your mom is always critical of men, you might form a belief that all men cannot be trusted. This will color your perception until hopefully you start to notice your patterns and reshape perceptions based on experiences. In order to have a healthy future relationship with a man, something will need to shift (if you want it to).

We don't have to keep repeating history. Repetition compulsion is not set in stone. We have the power to build resilience muscles, tapping into our innate capacity to live healthier and more fulfilled lives. But where do we start? We start by cultivating our ability to witness ourselves. You can learn to become more self-aware and intuitive, so you can shift your experience when and how it matters most.

Part Two

Becoming Your Own Guide

Chapter 4

Developing Self-Awareness and Intuition

In order to shift our perceptions and build healthier neural networks, we need to become more attuned to our inner world and those around us. Not everyone is naturally self-aware. Not everyone can understand others well. And that's okay. But if you're wondering whether you have self-awareness, the question itself shows you're already more self-aware than you might think. By retraining all your senses to become more aware of the things that set off your internal alarm bells, and tinkering with the way your brain interprets those incoming messages, you can consider exploring new perceptions that aren't anxious.

We are constantly "taking the temperature" of our surroundings. Our *felt sense* is the voice of that inner thermostat. It's an intuitive wisdom that helps us understand what's happening around us. When you feel anxious, you might experience sensations like stomach pains, heat, chills, racing heart, sweaty hands, or tingling. These are all messages from your body—sent through signals from the vagus nerve, heart, lungs, gut, muscles, and other body systems—alerting you to tune in to what's going on. (Siegel 2010).

But many of us were taught to ignore these important signals or, conversely, we learn to attach way too much meaning to them. We never learned to calibrate our systems properly, to nurture the fine balance of a healthy felt sense. It's important to listen to your body and develop your felt sense, so you can better understand what your body needs to be healthy and vibrant. You can repair your felt sense with EMDR-style activities. As you enhance self-awareness and unlock intuition, you will learn to trust your inner alarm system and tap into your body's innate wisdom.

Empathy and curiosity are the special tools that both encourage, and result from, a healthy, working "felt sense." Not everyone is naturally curious or empathetic, but the good news is that we can learn and practice these skills.

Cultivating Empathy

The word "empathy" might seem mushy-gushy soft, right? But becoming softer makes us tougher. It seems counterintuitive. The most meaningful truths usually are. *Empathy* is a superpower that you use to tune in to the needs of others and yourself. This connection helps repair any attachment challenges you tend to face. True empathy allows you to sprinkle your compassion generously, in just the right amount, while still maintaining emotional boundaries (because self-compassion is a big part of true empathy). It's a balanced mix of understanding others' needs and honoring your own. You can cultivate deep understanding of other people without letting it derail you and take over your inner world.

Growing Curiosity

Curiosity is having a hunger for the understanding required for empathy. You want to understand people without judging them? Become curious about *why* they might be reacting in this or that way. Grow curious about your own visceral reactions to certain relationship dynamics. You ultimately want to look deep inside your inner world without attaching too much emotion to it. Take objects of your curiosity seriously without taking them *too seriously*. It's like observing people as an anthropologist would, without *becoming* each culture they observe. They get involved just enough to maintain a sense of self while also bringing compassion and insight to those they observe. As you become more curious, you will unlock the door to self-awareness. On this journey to personal growth, curiosity and empathy go hand in hand.

Gaining Empowering Agency

Imagine ultimate power, feeling completely in control over your own life, as the hero of your own story. Bessel van der Kolk, a wise sage in the field of neuroscience, tells us that agency starts with perception. As you become more aware of your body sensations and embrace your felt sense, you start feeling more in control. The more control you feel, the more you will trust your inner wisdom. You'll start noticing that your intuition becomes more reliable and accurate (2015).

To develop empathy and curiosity, and ultimately agency, in this chapter we'll dive into exercises that can enhance your felt sense—a fancy term for being aware of what's going on inside your body. By honing your felt sense, you'll not only become more self-aware but also boost your capacity for empathy. It's a win-win! Then a sense of agency will empower you to take charge of your body and emotions in ways that make you a master of your destiny—by building a toolbox of resources and inner resonance. This journey unfolds within your own body.

Your Body Remembers

The body holds brilliant wisdom, and I encourage you to tap into your body's messaging as you develop more connection to it. Our memories, experiences, and emotions are stored not just in our mind, but are also embedded in the cells in our body too, through *cellular memory*. That's why sometimes we might feel "body sensations," which are body-based symptoms letting us know we're feeling anxiety or discomfort even when there's an absence of stressful or anxious thoughts. Our body is likely to remember something familiar and "tune in" before our mind and brain do.

Have you ever felt uncomfortable in your own skin, or not safe in certain situations, even when there's no apparent reason to feel this way? It could be because your body senses a lack of safety or confusing boundaries, and is sending you messages to check in with yourself. Throughout this book, you will learn techniques to help you tell the difference between a *trigger* and a *healthy gut feeling*.

Sometimes, you may feel uncomfortable in a situation where there is no obvious danger because your body is having a flashback. A *body flashback* is when your body is reminded of a past upsetting experience because something happening around you is triggering that emotional or somatic memory. A "part" of you is triggered and is doing its best to mobilize in order to protect you. If you're triggered and want to react due to a past memory, fear, or emotional flooding, this can cause you harm. Whenever you react to an objectively healthy situation or relationship with a fight, flight, or freeze response, you may jeopardize relationships or opportunities. Being triggered and thrown into a past memory or "part," brings perceptions that are maladaptive, like premonitions stemming from a muddled memory or emotion.

Other times, you can experience a "gut" feeling that something is off. It's a message that you may need to make a change. This is healthy bodily feedback that uses your felt sense to help you make wise choices.

You can begin to repair attachment patterns by tapping into your felt sense—noticing and connecting body sensations to your current experiences. It's like following a treasure map to find hidden connections. Your natural patterns, sensations, and energy flow hold the clues you need to repair your nervous system's wear and tear. They also show you what you need to pay attention to so you can make different choices in life.

Exploring Your Felt Sense

A felt sense is beyond the tangible. It's a somatic and energetic sense we all have and cultivating it builds deeper emotional literacy, beyond words. Your ability to recognize your natural patterns, sensations, and energy flow helps trace and repair any frayed connections in your nervous system.

An emotion or a feeling is relatively easier to label and identify than a felt sense. Consider the following examples. Notice how, with a feeling, there is cause and effect.

- "I feel hurt and lonely because none of my friends are calling me back."

- "I feel overwhelmed because my mom always comes over without calling first."

- "I feel betrayed because you told my boss something I said to you in confidence."

Let's look at those feeling scenarios again, this time through a felt-sense lens.

Your friends aren't calling you back: You feel familiar feelings of rejection or abandonment. It's likely that your friends have a lot going on in their lives and it's nothing personal. You logically understand that, but your body is telling you a different story. Familiar sensations inside you might be described as raw, light-headed, and cloudy. Alternately, your friends aren't calling you back and there is a chance that one is upset at you. She's sending confusing messages that you want to clarify.

Your mom has no boundaries: You feel familiar feelings of overwhelm and resentment. It's likely you had no idea what boundaries were growing up, let alone how to set and maintain healthy ones. Perhaps you became a people pleaser and are afraid to tell people your needs. When your mom walks in unannounced, you have familiar reactions inside your body, similar to all those times you pushed beyond your limits to make people happy—but always felt resentful. Maybe you feel a heaviness in your stomach and chest. Or a choking feeling, like something is closing in on your throat. Maybe your palms start to sweat or you have an ache in the back of your eye.

Your coworker betrayed your trust: Your coworker told your boss something you had said to them in confidence. It wasn't *that* big a deal, so why are you feeling rage? Your body might react as if your coworker literally stabbed you in the back, with a sense of frozenness and prickliness in your back. Your face likely feels hot and your heart won't stop racing. Plus, you feel a sense of overwhelming shame for "overreacting."

Tapping into your felt sense will help you discover whether the anxiety you're feeling is related to your past experiences, or there's a real concern that needs to be addressed. Once you process the sensitive emotions related to the past, by filtering out the past from present-day emotions and experiences, you'll be able to communicate in a calmer, less reactive way. Then you'll feel clearer about what needs to be addressed with your friend, mother, or coworker.

These are all examples of felt sense. Focusing on felt sense allows us to identify the nuances that weigh on our feelings without digging too much into painful details of the associated memories. Unlike other therapies, we don't even have to visit those old stories in full detail because with felt sense, we are looking for the body's reaction to whatever version of the story is coming up. While learning to name the emotions we feel can be really helpful at the beginning of our emotional literacy journey, it will only take us so far. A felt sense like heaviness or frozenness is actually way less intense than feeling emotions like anger, bitterness, or embarrassment. It helps diffuse the intensity and bring it down to a more tolerable level, which makes processing an emotion a lot more tolerable. When we process a felt sense, we usually feel a release inside.

Becoming more aware of felt sense can be liberating. It can become a new way to relate to the world, and yourself, that opens a window offering a clearer view of what's going on. It's like getting glasses that you never knew you needed, and finally seeing things as they are. When we are self-healing, it is much gentler to work with felt sense.

Here are four steps for cultivating emotional literacy. If you would like more support, you can download information on the process at http://www.integrativepsych.co/emdrforanxiety.

1. At any given time, name the obvious emotions you are feeling.

2. Start to notice where those feelings are felt in your body.

3. Find just the right word to describe the nuance of your emotion.

4. When you name all the nuanced emotions out loud, allow the pent-up energy to release.

A felt sense is simply an attuned awareness of your internal state. Here are some of the ways to find words describing sensations involved. As you notice an emotion, consider these qualities to come up with your own word that captures it.

Feeling Sensations

- Pressure
- Breeze of air
- Tension
- Pain
- Tingling or numbness
- Itching
- Temperature

Sensory Input from the Five Senses

- Sound
- Taste
- Smell
- Touch
- Sight (If your eyes are closed, you can use your "mind's eye," or imagination's vision.)

Other Observations

- Size
- Shape
- Heaviness or lightness
- Motion (Can be a pattern or ongoing.)
- Speed
- Texture
- Color
- Mood, feeling, emotion
- Absence of something, emptiness

Associations with the Elements

- Fire
- Water
- Earth
- Air

Each sensation has descriptions that can be even subtler than these examples. Many of us need to actively relearn how to feel sensations in our body, after years of tuning them out. Don't feel discouraged if it's not so easy. Feeling body sensations can seem strange or hard, and that is okay. It's totally normal. As long as you feel able to explore your felt sense, go for it. Just the willingness to try staying present in your body is a positive step!

To support this, here's an activity you can do daily or whenever you have time. It will develop attunement toward your felt sense. Exercising and developing this form of emotional intelligence will be important for your ability to self-administer EMDR.

Exercise: Felt-Sense Body Scan

As you begin this felt-sense meditation, please proceed with caution and stop if it begins to feel like too much. Some people who have experienced trauma have a hard time connecting to their bodies in this way, as it can feel like ripping open a wound that has barely scabbed over. That's not what we want. If this exercise causes you to feel significantly worse, please pause here and reach out to a trauma specialist before continuing with this book.

If you engage a traumatized, or unbearably intense, part of your body during this exercise, gently shift your awareness toward a neutral or relaxed part instead. Any time you have a particularly intense session, do a grounding exercise from chapter 8 immediately after this meditation.

This body scan can be done daily, or even a few times throughout the day. It's a very healthy practice that will fit any schedule, so do it whenever possible. Each time you do this activity, pay attention to ever subtler sensations. Here are the steps.

1. Sit or lie down in a quiet place where you can comfortably focus without disruption. Take a few minutes to notice the sensations in your body.

2. Start at the bottom of your toes and notice the sensations. Sit mindfully and observe. Continue on to the bottom of your

foot, then the top of your foot. Keep moving up, limb by limb, noticing what is going on inside for a few moments. If you feel an uncomfortable sensation in a particular spot, try to just notice it without willing it away. Take note of its qualities. Breathe into the area deeply, then exhale for as long as you can. Then move on to the next body part. Keep going until your attention has reached the top of your head.

3. Take a deep breath and give yourself time to reorient to your surroundings. You may feel like you are just waking up from a nap, so give yourself a moment. If the session was difficult or intense, follow up with a grounding and reorienting exercise from chapter 8.

As you continue to practice the body scan, track your progress inside your journal. You can draw a picture of a body and write words or draw with colors to represent different sensations. More tools to support your practice are included in the Emotional Literacy Primer, which you can download at http://www .integrativepsych.co/emdrforanxiety. They include a body scan template you can use for tracking and a body scan meditation video.

Developing your felt sense and attunement skills is key to healing and breaking unhealthy patterns. EMDR relies on self-awareness and intuition, which are developed by connecting with emotions *and* sensations. This can guide you to discover the different parts that make you who you are. As you get to know these parts and the relationship dynamics that helped those parts come to be, you will be better equipped to correct your natural tendency toward repetition compulsion. Growing self-awareness leads to charting a new course that creates stronger, healthier neural networks. Now let's lean into the parts that carry your anxiety burdens.

Chapter 5

Get to Know Your Anxious Parts

During our early years, we were vulnerable and completely dependent on primary caregivers to meet our basic needs for safety, security, and protection. As time went on, our needs became more adaptive and complex, but we still relied on support from—and connection with—some sort of primary attachment figure. In addition to our basic physical needs for water, food, air, and so on, all humans need bare minimum emotional basics like connection, attunement, trust, autonomy, love, and eventually sexuality (Heller and LaPierre 2012), integrity, appreciation, and self-expression (Peyton 2017).

A child with strong attachments is more likely to feel comfortable exploring their environment independently and will usually be more socially savvy. But if a child carries underlying feelings of abandonment, confusion, being misunderstood, they are more likely to grow up with anxiety and show maladaptive behaviors. These anxious feelings are likely to continue expanding until a sense of secure attachment is restored. If not tended to, anxiety can worsen over time and become depression or an anxiety-related disorder.

When it comes to regarding your caregivers, know that we're generally imperfect humans. Caregivers just have to be "good enough" at parenting, meaning, they don't have to be perfect in order to be successful at raising healthy, resilient children. Nobody is perfect (Winnicott 1991). As Brené Brown expresses in her books and podcasts, *everyone does the best they can with the tools they are given.* Even the most well-intentioned parents can't be everything to everyone.

Regardless of the quality of our upbringing, eventually, when we are old enough, we need to take responsibility for our own destiny.

It's normal if you want to resolve your attachment wounds via a two-way street, processing the hurt with the person who let you down. When that's possible, you may find satisfaction and validation through their accountability or apology. However, it may not be possible to include parents or caregivers in your healing process. You can achieve closure and relief, but it will take a different form of processing. When you work on strengthening self-energy, and become more empowered, the need for direct restitution becomes less alluring or needed.

As a therapist, my goal is to empower clients to anchor themselves with a secure relationship. At first, a therapist might become a stand-in attachment figure. Any healthy, consistent, respectful relationship will help reinforce a stronger, secure template. Whether that anchor is a therapist, mentor, or friend, they can provide a mental and somatic model for you to cultivate your own inner secure attachment figure, who can be there for your inner child. When you work on your own attachment repairs by providing your "child parts" with a healthy replacement relationship, shifts and healing naturally occur.

This book is focused on a self-healing process in which you play a dual role in your own healing. You will cultivate a part of self that can take on the parental figure that you needed as a child. Let's look more closely at the support you didn't receive.

The Adventure of Growing Up

Looking back on your formative years, you may notice areas that lacked support, which created "stuck points" at various stages. Understanding these will help you zero in on how to focus your growth efforts and identify "parts" you want to work with. Knowing the stages of development that are *meant* to take place is important, as is knowing the basic needs we are meant to have.

Erik Erikson's theory of psychosocial development creates a roadmap for this work (1959–1982). Just like we master physical skills like crawling, walking, or riding a bike, Erikson says we also need to master some social and emotional skills to be successful. To be well-rounded, healthy adults, we need to master each stage of development just like we graduate from different levels of school when we accomplish academic goals. It's never too late to fix things, because we can always go back and try to master a stage again. So even though things like being anxious when speaking publicly, or finding it hard to make friends, may seem to be aspects of who we are, according to Erikson, they might instead be signs that we need to go back and revisit an earlier stage. As adults, we can go back and heal the parts of us that didn't have basic needs met back then.

Using this timeline, you can identify relationship dynamics that may have led to the formation of a particular part, offering a history of where your auto-responses may have originated from. Don't worry, you are not doomed if you never passed some of the earlier stages. If we don't pass one level, we still move on to the next one, but we may be missing some critical skills that for our personality and relationships. It could make the following stages harder to navigate, but we can always go back to correct this.

Here is a summary of these stages that will help you explore any parts of you that may still be affected. What did, or didn't, you learn growing up?

Stage 1: Basic Trust vs. Mistrust (HOPE)— Infancy, 0–18 months

At this stage, our main challenge is learning to rely on others. This is when the seeds of trusting relationships are born, creating a foundation for future social connections. Hopefully it's when we start to trust a caregiver who's consistently there for us, responding to our needs and making us feel secure. Trust is not usually dependent on the quantity of attention we get, but the quality of an attuned connection with our primary caregiver. For example, say you were a newborn who spent a few months in intensive care. Your parents could only be there with you for a few hours a day, but when they were there they were *all-in*. That could be enough for you to develop trust in people. Even if a parent couldn't be there, but a caring nurse was able to make the you feel warm and fuzzy for a time, that could be enough for you to form an intrinsic sense of security that humans will show up for you and won't hurt you.

Infants are naturally intuitive and sense who they can trust. When we are provided with stable and constant care as an infant, when we are a bit older and start to interact with other people, we show preferences toward our trustworthy caregivers. The idea isn't that we should learn to trust everyone. The goal is that we will learn to be trusting, yet discerning, in a balanced way. Navigating this stage successfully helps us learn to trust others and ourselves later in life. When development during these years lags, we might believe the world is scary and unpredictable, so we develop anxious "parts" with feelings of uneasiness, fear, and mistrust. On the other hand, if a healthy internal alarm system was never established, we might develop "parts" that trust too easily—even people who should not be trusted. When this stage is graduated effectively, we will develop a hopeful, trusting attitude toward other people, ourselves, and the world at large while also being cautious around iffy people and complete strangers.

Stage 2: Autonomy vs. Shame (WILL)—Early Childhood, 1–3 years old

This is when we begin making some of our own choices. In this stage, we take initial steps toward independence and perform basic tasks "all by ourselves" in a gentle, protected, guided way. We may fall sometimes, but we have already learned to *trust* that our caregiver will be there to pick us up when we fall. If they are overprotective and don't let us fail sometimes, we might develop anxious "parts" who don't believe they are capable of doing things on their own.

If caregivers are completely inattentive, overly strict, or punishing, some anxious "parts" might develop shame and self-doubt. During this stage, we are encouraged to explore talents, abilities, and "big kid" activities such as toileting or helping wash dishes. Expectations are set, like brushing teeth or cleaning up toys, that we are lovingly encouraged to meet independently. We must be given the encouragement and freedom to explore, but also have a safe space in which failures are normalized. Attentive caregivers may say things like, "Oh no! You fell down. I can see you are really sad. Let's try again when you are ready!" or "Oops, you had an accident. It's okay. It takes time to learn to make it to the potty on time. When your body feels ready, you will know."

The following will have negative long-term outcomes: harsh punishments, constant corrections, overcompensation, overprotection, empty praise, ridicule, threats for not doing what is expected, and reprimands for expressing emotions like "Don't be like that" or "Stop crying!" If your caregivers used any of these, take note for when we explore self-parenting in chapter 6. When caregivers punish a child trying to explore autonomy, it can form "parts" with long-term feelings of shame, incompetence, and doubt. If this stage is graduated effectively, a child will develop a strong will and healthy self-control.

Stage 3: Initiative vs. Guilt (PURPOSE)— Preschool Years, ages 3–5

During the preschool years, we learn to do things completely on our own. This is unlike the previous stage, when caregivers are always there to catch us when we fall. Allowing children to take initiative and make choices about how they dress themselves, who they want to play with, which activities they want to do, and how they interact with peers will further develop confidence and effective leadership skills. Even if there are potential consequences.

If we are rarely allowed to make these decisions, we can develop anxious "parts" that feel shame or like they are a burden to others. When parents are overly involved, we feel incapable of doing things on their own and grow anxious. "Parts" develop adaptive skills to get through these challenges and protect our "self." In adulthood, some signs of unsupported needs at this stage include becoming a follower, putting aside one's own needs to fit in, or the opposite—becoming a bully to prove something. Both extremes create challenging social dynamics and vicious cycles that lead to unhealthy shame.

This is also a typical stage for inquiry. We ask lots of questions to help build knowledge of the world around us. If our questions are met with criticism, annoyance, and condescension, we might develop anxious "parts" that feel withdrawn or embarrassed, or think things aren't worth trying. When this stage is graduated effectively, we develop a healthy, strong sense of purpose in this world. If not, we might question our worthiness and develop a compromised sense of self.

Stage 4: Industry vs. Inferiority (COMPETENCE)—Elementary Years, ages 6–11

During this stage, it's typical for us to compare our self-worth to others. Classrooms tend to have hierarchies, and we might start to notice major differences in personal abilities and how they compare to other children. In the previous stages, parents and caregivers played a central role, but in this challenge a teacher can also make or break our successful development. A teacher can either stand up for a child who faces discrimination or a sense of inferiority, or they can contribute to the problem. Think back to this stage in your life, and identify defining moments when a teacher either built you up, or tore you down, as you attempted to find your way in social and academic environments. A neglectful teacher can lead to forming an anxious "part" with feelings of inferiority or self-doubt.

Our peer group is incredibly important to this stage of development as well. As we start to try and prove ourselves in areas that seem important to others and society, we can develop a sense of security and ease as we do things we are good at. By encouraging a realistic sense of accomplishment, feelings of competency in achieving independent goals increase. But teachers and parents who push tasks and hobbies that are too advanced or not within our comfort zone might inadvertently foster the formation of "parts" with a sense of incompetency or self-doubt, and a reluctance to try new things in the future.

If this stage is graduated effectively, we will develop a strong drive and healthy sense of competence. We will feel secure in the knowledge that making a mistake is not a colossal failure, and that trying again will eventually result in success. We might even learn to see each fall as benign, or even a positive thing that could lead to a different path. It might build up our resilience muscles for future challenges. We remain curious about new possibilities.

Stage 5: Identity vs. Role Confusion (FIDELITY)—Teenage Years, ages 12–18

As an adolescent, it is completely normal and healthy to question our sense of self. We ask big questions: "Who am I?" "Where am I going in life?" "How do I fit into the bigger picture?" Adolescents embark on an exploratory journey to find our own unique identity. At this stage, we evaluate personal or religious beliefs, values, morals, and life goals independent of our parent's choices. If parents, teachers, or other significant people in our life allow this healthy exploration, we will eventually determine our own identity in a safe and healthy way. If they continually push conformity, shaming the child for this normal human process, and choose to stifle our independence and autonomy, we will likely face some sort of identity confusion. This can lead to a range of issues like a crisis of faith, teen rebellion, leaving home too early, gender confusion, and in extreme cases, suicidal ideation. As teens, we search for a sense of community and belonging as we start to develop the need to fit in. Someone who hasn't graduated this stage might face existential maladaptive feelings that they are different from everyone and that they don't belong anywhere. They might feel that no matter what they do, they will not be good enough. Or they might choose to become estranged from others to preempt being rejected. Not many of us begin our challenges at this stage. Usually, we have to dig back further and work to graduate from a previous stage before we can have the stable footing we need to properly heal in this stage.

Stage 6: Intimacy vs. Isolation (LOVE)—Adult Years, ages 18–40

In this first stage of adult development, dating, marriage or partnership, building a family, and establishing friendships is the primary focus. It will hopefully lead to experiences of love and intimacy. Striving for security and hope will support the ability to form lasting relationships. When there is a sense of safety, caring, and commitment in foundational relationships, as a healthy adult we can successfully resolve crises of intimacy and feelings of isolation—even if we don't have a life partner. No matter our relationship status, when we achieve this stage we'll find satisfaction in many different types of relationships. As we get older, we tend to recognize the importance of having a variety of relationship connections. We realize that intimacy is not simple and revisit relationship goals. If we graduate this stage, we'll find love and satisfaction within each type of relationship, even when we inevitably long for other types of relationships.

Stage 7: Generativity vs. Stagnation (CARE)— Middle Age Years, ages 40–65

At this stage, we generally feel settled in our lives, having already identified what is and is not important to us. It is a normal time for transition, reevaluating career paths and questioning what we want to do indefinitely. During this time, adults appreciate their relationships with children and grandchildren more, and seek out activities that foster a greater sense of purpose. Volunteer work, finding meaningful ways to contribute to society, and increasing job productivity are all signs of healthy graduation from this stage. If we regret past choices, and feel like we are stagnating, we might feel an overwhelming sense of uselessness and lack of purpose. Reparations involve a commitment to change, as well as greater efforts at self-care and finding new purpose.

Stage 8: Ego Integrity vs. Despair (WISDOM)— Elder Years, ages 65+

When we reach the ages of 65 and beyond, we recognize that this is the last chapter of life. Retirement is on the horizon or has already taken place. At this stage, we gain ego-integrity and wisdom by accepting of life's victories, defeats, accomplishments, and lack of accomplishments. We experience appreciation of life's process. Through understanding the nature of life and death, we feel at peace with whatever the future holds. When this stage is not experiences in a healthy way, we might feel tortured with guilt about the past or feel bad about not fulfilling certain accomplishments or goals. This can lead to a sad state of hopelessness and deep depression. Successful graduation of this stage brings a sense of accomplishment, inner peace, heightened wisdom, and gratitude for a well-lived life.

After reading about these psychosocial developmental stages, can you identify points where you might have become stuck, perhaps unable to learn some of these skills? I encourage you to think of these as parts of yourself that you can now tend. If this is challenging for you to visualize, I encourage you to watch the Disney movie *Inside Out*. It offers a great sense of what different parts of ourselves might act like inside the brain. Most of the movie takes place in an eleven-year-old girl's head. Riley was born with two parts, Joy and Sadness. As she grows through the developmental stages, Anger, Fear, and Disgust join her internal family. This movie helps us visualize how it's possible for different parts inside our head can interact with each other and even cause a bit of drama.

Like Riley, we all have different parts inside that represent different emotions, experiences, tendencies, tools, and reactions. They help shape our personality. When we are babies, we only have a few parts and they each have very basic functions. As we grow, and life circumstances happen, more parts join the internal family in order to help out. Some join the family to protect us, and others join to help fix things when they go wrong. When we go through something traumatic or neglectful, sometimes parts will freeze in time and hide deep inside the "dungeon" of our unconscious. The other parts work really hard to protect those more fragile parts and help keep them safe, tucked deep below the conscious mind. Now that you can see yourself as a system of parts, let's explore how they can work together for healing.

A Family of Internal Parts

In his therapy practice, psychologist Richard C. Schwartz saw that it was helpful for clients to creatively visualize their subpersonalities, or parts, as if they were an actual family. He found that once all of the "family members" were identified, healing became a sort of group therapy inside the psyche. This process is led by a part known as the *core self*, whose role is to parent all the parts.

When anxiety happens, it's usually because one or more parts are triggered and acting out, likely going head-to-head with each other. Alarm bells start to ring in the body. This internal conflict wreaks havoc on the nervous system. Imagine what would happen if a group of firefighters never trained to work together as a group. In a state of emergency, they would bump into each other, double up on jobs meant for one person, or drop the ball on essential tasks. The core self is like the fire chief who makes sure everyone trains together, uses their skills properly, and works cohesively.

This method, known as internal family systems (IFS), helps us become more self-aware and self-compassionate as we develop an appreciation for each part—both as an individual part and how they interact with other parts. We learn to see that the part's behaviors make sense given how and when they were formed inside us, during a particular stage of development. Basically, the part did not get what they needed back then, so they adapted the best they could at the time. This part was there for us when that adaptation was the only way to get through. We can learn to be grateful for the amazing job each part did in the past, and we can help them evolve into new roles. Now that we have grown up, those old reactions have become maladaptive. As adults, we can take control and give our parts more mature responses or assure the parts that the core self, or self-parent, will handle things.

This can function like a real-life family, where people have conflict and the more dominant ones rule. The family members who are the "squeaky wheels" get heard. A parent without parenting skills, and likewise a leader without leadership skills, does not have a very cohesive group around them. As our internal family grows, the more dominant parts can start to take over the self, if we are not emotionally healthy (Early 2009). When we are anxious or dysregulated, the calm and logical messages of our core self are muffled. While all of our inner parts are loudly fighting for attention and control, it's hard to hear a voice of reason. We have a feeling that we are off-track, that parts of us need firm, gentle support to get them playing nicely together once again. Here's how Andrea describes her internal family of parts.

I imagine a superhero part that is most dominant. She tries to be in charge of all the other parts. She is basically Wonder Woman with many arms, so she can do everything at once. She works full time, cooks and cleans, drives carpool, is the first one to volunteer in the community, and takes care of her aging grandmother while also raising a houseful of children. She has dinner on the table, even on soccer nights. This protective part gets easily frustrated when she encounters blips in her plans and when things don't go her way. She has angry outbursts and is short tempered. She thinks that sleep is for the weak. But she is verbally abusive to weaker parts that can't keep up with her.

I also have a little-child part who seems really young, maybe seven or eight years old. When the superhero part is done with her meltdowns and realizes she can't keep up with all the unrealistic expectations she sets for herself, this child part emerges and cries. My exiled child part never feels like she is enough, for anyone. Wonder Woman works hard to protect this "weak" child part from emerging.

There is a father figure in my internal family who is a goofy-looking bear with a polka dot vest and a big smile. He sometimes steps in when my kids are around and need a more relaxed and fun-loving persona. When this silly reactive part emerges, Wonder Woman hates it. I often feel a tug-of-war inside, between the two of them: the responsible, bossy, tightly wound side and the fun loving, carefree, goofy, clown side.

I also have this old-fashioned, older woman part who looks like she is carrying a bunch of shopping bags. I haven't really gotten to know her yet, but I assume she is there to take care of my younger parts. She seems motherly.

As I explained to Andrea, the goal is not necessarily to give her Wonder Woman part a break. It's to strengthen her inner core self, her spiritual center, so that she no longer relies on these parts. She is an adult now, with the tools to "drive her own bus," set boundaries and more realistic expectations, while her internal family remains safely in the passenger seats.

Imagine that your core self is the adult driver of a school bus full of children fighting for attention. A responsible adult would never hand over the wheel to a child. But that's what you are doing when you let your child parts get so strong that they take over your mind. With the parts work you'll do in this book, you can give the core self tools to take back the wheel. Your core self can become a brilliant inner parent who can help settle the inner children down and continue to drive through life with more calm and control. Through the parts work in the next chapter, you will learn to gently and skillfully lead your inner family to a healthy state of cohesion. The goal is to help strengthen your core self so you can be the leader of your own inner world.

Chapter 6

Lead the Wounded Parts of You

The core self is your rightful team leader. When chaos and challenges hit, if the core self isn't strong and healthy, their voice is drowned out in the crowd. The result is internal conflict—essentially, anxiety. In this chapter, you will learn to access the core self, do a little leadership training, and gently take back control of all the parts. This will foster a sense of emotional well-being, deep down inside you. With a little support, your parts will have an effective leader who can successfully coach them and help them navigate all of life's ups and downs.

When embodied and strengthened, our core self has the capacity to bring balance and cohesion to our whole internal system of parts. Every person has one, even if the voice is currently drowned out by the loud voices and intense energy of all the other parts. As the core self becomes stronger, we have a greater capacity to help all the other parts find newer, more adaptive roles as well as a fresh sense of purpose. With more of this *self-energy*, we reparent all the parts, improving the way we nurture, treat, and value ourselves (and others as well). This skill-building exercise is known as *self-leadership training*.

Getting to Know Your Core Self

The core self is like the conductor of an orchestra. It leads all the other parts and guides them to play harmoniously together. It is untouched by trauma and is not influenced by any of the chaos around them. It is also not triggered into reactivity, like the other parts are. Like a conductor, the core self can distance from all the background chaos of the crowd and all the different instruments playing at once—all to stay in the zone. Wouldn't it be nice to be able to do that all the time? Even when the voice of the core self seems drowned out by the noise of all the other parts, no matter what, the self maintains its essential qualities. This means there will always be hope. You can always find your way back to your core self. It helps to strengthen your self-energy by consciously engaging the qualities inherent to your core self. Sometimes these qualities need to be modeled by an experienced therapist or mentor until your self-energy gets a bit stronger.

The core self is basically you at your best, owning your job as leader of your inner world, helping to channel the strengths of each part in more advanced ways. It's your healthy parasympathetic nervous system, your highly toned vagus nerve. It involves gratitude and recognition for the parts that have been there for you through thick and thin. With a mature core self, your parts will grow and mature too. It supports the restructuring of inner roles to keep internal dynamics safe and fulfilling. Ultimately, each part can feel a sense of belonging and purpose within the family system. Feeling good and in your groove is a sign that your parts are getting along and working together as a strong team.

Underneath your collection of parts, your true core self—what some call your "spiritual center"—is whole and complete. By strengthening your core qualities of self, you will be able to heal your parts and guide them to learn new tools. Let's look at these qualities. Then we'll explore three common types of parts in depth, so your core self knows the exact inner-family dynamics they are leading.

Core Self-Leadership Qualities

You can easily distinguish your core self from the other parts by its leadership qualities. When we are self-led, we can more easily and expeditiously CHIP away the layers to reveal core-self qualities. I offer you the following expanded acronym to describe these qualities of self (Anderson 2021).

C: Compassionate, Confident, Courageous, Connected, Curious, Clear, Calm, Creative

H: Hopeful, Humble, Harmonious, Humorous, Honest

I: Introspective, Inviting, Innovative

P: Playful, Patient, Perspective, Persistent, Pleasant

When you are using these core-self qualities to engage with other parts, you will know that you are leading in self-mode. You can download more information about what these qualities truly mean and how you can cultivate them at http://www.integrativepsych.co/emdrfor anxiety.

It's often tricky to distinguish between the core self and another part. Some parts are protective and seem dominating as they try to maintain control or guard another part. Some of the parts that formed when you were young may be based on the character traits of significant people in your life, who may have had maladaptive responses themselves. While they were technically adults at the time of their influence on you, they may have been operating from an ungraduated state of development, not equipped to model adaptive tools for you.

When you are leading from the core self, there will be inner peace and no other part will feel shut down. All the parts will work cohesively for the greater good of the inner family and they will each be supported. In their quest to heal, they will actualize their potential and feel seen, heard, understood, and valued by you.

Look at the core qualities of the CHIP list. Explore qualities that you feel you have naturally. Select the ones that have been more difficult to learn. Do you have these qualities in all circumstances, at specific times, or with specific people? When you are observing yourself, do you maintain those qualities? For example, you may find it a lot easier to have compassion or hope for others. But those qualities are lacking when you look inward. Keep the qualities of the core self in mind as we look more deeply at the other parts it leads.

Exiled Parts—Vulnerable Keepers of Painful Memories

Our vulnerable child parts are the keepers of all painful memories and emotions. They are the parts shoved down, deep into the "dungeons" of our unconscious minds. These parts have been exiled for various reasons, usually to protect you from harm. Born out of harmful self-perceptions and shame, most often these parts are the background noise, worries, fears, and emotions that make us feel child-like. Other parts you will soon learn about do everything in their power to prevent the child parts from reaching your conscious mind. But once your self-energy is strengthened, you can identify and connect with your exiled child parts, and help them heal proactively. As you start to understand the implications of attachment and psychosocial development, you can better recognize their ages and developmental stages. Here are ways you can identify an exile part.

- They seem frozen in time, as wounded and exiled parts freeze at the age they experienced emotional neglect or pain. Their reactions demonstrate the emotional maturity of their frozen age.

- They are holding on to something from the past, like a warped perception or a burden.

- When triggered, they react in extreme and desperate ways. This is an effort to be seen, cared for, and given a chance to tell their story. Their reactions will resemble yours, at that age.

- After contact with them, you are left feeling fragile and vulnerable. You might feel emotionally flooded.

- You sense a pull, and perhaps mixed emotions. This can indicate that other parts are trying to guard them, fearing that their emotions will overtake you and flood your system.

To truly heal, exiled parts must feel validated, comforted, and safe without protection from other parts. They need to learn to trust you, the core self, and your ability to parent, safeguard, manage, and support them. In self-mode, you need to show them genuine, unconditional love and appreciation. Imagine a little child holding a fifty-pound weight. When an exile is unburdened, you can lift that weight from the part's chest, back, or wherever your body tends to carry burdens. Without this extra weight, the exiled part will start to shift their anxieties and soften. It might take some time, and quite a few check-ins, but eventually the wounded child part will start to feel a lot less tired, a lot more playful, and will be ready to mature to the next developmental stage.

When you are triggered, do you recognize any qualities of an exiled part in yourself? If yes, take some notes. They will be helpful in later activities. What kinds of circumstances trigger you?

First Responder Parts—Reactive and Protective Forces

Protective parts tend to guard the exiled parts. While broadly known as "firefighters," I like to call these parts *first responders*. Beyond putting out fires, they respond to anything they perceive as a threat or an emergency in quick and impulsive ways. They have learned to do everything they can to defend and settle down the exiled parts, tucking them back into the unconscious in the most adaptive way they can. As adults, if we haven't yet learned new tools, our reactive responder parts might numb out or distract to protect an exiled part from feeling uncomfortable emotions. They do this by working too much, sleeping too much, or engaging in excessive, obsessive, addictive behaviors. In extreme cases they might even self-harm, be violent, dissociate, or zone out through fantasizing or playing video games instead of functioning in the world. If you've been experiencing any of these behaviors for extended periods of time, it may be helpful to reach out to a mental health professional.

Our first-responder parts smell danger and fear from a mile away. They are preprogrammed to react in whatever way will make things better for us, in the moment. They are not concerned about long-term repercussions. These are our defense mechanisms, our pain numbers, our shut-down modes, and our autopilot responses. They will use any other emergency reaction they have at their disposal. It's like a wannabe firefighter who sees a big fire through a window, so they impulsively break down the door of the house, knock over furniture, and flood the house with water. When it's all over and you assess the damage to the house, you realizes that the fire was actually controlled inside a large fireplace. Oops. There was no need to ruin all the furniture and break the doorframe after all. I think we can all relate to acting impulsively on autopilot, thinking we are helping in the moment—then realizing we caused more harm than good.

These reactive parts are also in charge of cleaning up messes. They think quickly and get the job done on the spot, without thinking through what they are about to do. These first responders offer the qualities people love about us when there are urgent problems to solve and people to save. But without boundaries or pausing to gain foresight, we tend to create more problems than we solve (not necessarily for others, but definitely for ourselves).

With your help, these parts can learn to self-regulate before acting and they can learn healthier ways to respond to crisis situations (like making sure a fire is a real threat before trying to put it out with extreme measures). You know you are operating in reactive protective mode when:

- You respond to people or situations impulsively or errati-cally: saying things you don't mean and later regretting it, lying, yelling, screaming, hitting, slamming doors, throw-ing tantrums, or other over-the-top reactions.

- Your body experiences symptoms of panic, such as increased heartrate, hypervigilance, digestive problems, and body pains.

- You attempt to deal with stressful situations by using chemical substances, overeating or undereating, overexer-cising, hurting yourself, numbing, or acting out in other ways.

- You try anything and everything, even extreme measures, to extinguish thoughts, feelings, body sensations, memories, or images.

- Your reactions come out too fast, without thinking about them.

- You try to "put out a fire" in your relationships, but just keep making things worse and worse, as if you're pouring fuel on the fire. You have absolutely no idea why you are not making things better.

Inner turmoil, external conflict, or trying to fix problems in ways that create new problems indicate that a first responder is likely attempting to fix things on impulse. Like a real firefighter, it feels the need to act fast—do anything to make something stop or go, to fix it. But the quick fixes make problems worse. With this erratic, impulsive behavior, you can easily confuse a first-responder part with the underdeveloped immaturity of an exiled part. They also be confused with the core self, when their qualities are high-functioning. Because reactive, first-responder parts are in charge of cleaning up messes, from a young age you may have learned to be quite good at it. For example, if you were raised by an emotionally immature or needy parent, you probably took on a caretaking role of reacting to their needs. Role reversals like this can cause a lot of deep-rooted pain for a child. You may have grown up continuing that reactive caregiver role in your adult relationships. But you can learn to strengthen your sense of self.

Your core self's job will be to discern the first-responder part's reactions that you have learned over time, then give them newer, more adaptive strategies. Only then can you identify and help heal the exiled parts they have been protecting. For example, say you have a fear of being alone. Every person you have ever loved has either died, checked out emotionally, or left you. You will have exiled parts who are holding memories beneath this fear. Now imagine that you are expecting your partner to meet you at home after the workday, as usual. He is now three hours late and is not picking up his phone. You have called him about forty times. Your manager parts are out of ideas, so you are on the verge of a complete meltdown. Your strongest first-responder reaction has always been binge eating when your exiled feelings of abandonment are triggered. Although logically you know that eating two tubs of ice cream and an entire bag of cookies is not helpful, this first responder part swings into action, trying to distract you from emotionally breaking down by feeding you comfort food.

First responders need to be recognized and appreciated for their dedication over the years. Many of them were there during really tough times, saving you with skills they learned to help when you were younger. They helped you avoid all kinds of danger and helped get your needs met.

As an adult, when you know you are safe, first responders can learn newer, more mature, less destructive ways to solve problems. They no longer need to drown out the pain with food or drugs, or distract you with work or video games, because the wounded-child parts they protected have grown up and are okay with the discomforts of normal life. They can be content in the moment, experiencing life in a connected and mindful way. They can channel their reactive natures towards other, more heroic qualities, such as balanced amounts of courage, resilience, bravery, activism, and efficiency.

Do you recognize any qualities of first-responder parts when you are triggered? What types of impulsive reactions do you tend to enact? Think of some adaptive ways you've evolved over the years that have allowed your responses to become productive and helpful.

Manager and Controller Parts— Hardworking Proactive Protection

We have parts known as "managers" that are the controllers of every situation in our lives. Their mission is to actively prevent exiled parts from ever feeling hurt, rejected, or any sort of undesirable emotion. They don't wait for issues to come about, as their anxieties help them prevent pain proactively. The manager parts guide us and protect us from emotional discomfort and getting hurt in relationships. Over time, they learned to take charge or shut down as needed. They are workaholics that help us meet deadlines, rule followers that prevent us from getting into trouble, and rebels protecting us from being taken advantage of by others. They manifest as perfectionists, bosses, controllers, caregivers, judges, pessimists, planners, self-critics, and more. Counterintuitively, they might use avoidance and prevention strategies they learned in childhood. However, as they grow they need to learn new skills in order to be balanced, healthy, and adaptive.

Manager parts tend to be short-sighted, black-and-white thinkers that don't recognize the bigger picture or the tremendous value of other parts around them (in the Disney movie *Inside Out*, the character Joy has these qualities). With their one-track mind, managers can be hurtful without realizing it and cause pain to our internal system as well as in our relationships. They usually have a false sense of security in their ability to manage everything. They tend to try to dominate the self and ignore warning signs such as the emotions and body triggers that signal alarm bells in the brain and body (to the detriment of our nervous system).

With your help, these parts can learn to be more attuned to your needs. They can become nurturing, accepting, and communicative. You know that you are dealing with a manager when:

- You want to control or fix other people as a way to distract yourself from dealing with your own issues.

- You need to always be busy, avoiding situations and activities that require you to be emotionally present.

- You go to extreme efforts to either organize and clean, or avoid cleaning and even hoard things.

- You are obsessed with success or power in an extreme way.

- You have body symptoms, like tension, pain, muscle constriction, breath constriction, body rigidity, and even illnesses that flare up unexpectedly. These symptoms usually arise when stress occurs because the manager part constantly tries to control and avoids showing signs of weakness.

- You prioritize people pleasing over self-care, which manifests as a lack of boundaries, avoiding confrontation, or not wanting to deal with someone's disappointed in you.

- You avoid situations or people more than usual, as the manager part is preventing an exiled part from being triggered. This is likely due to a fear of imperfection or external criticism.

Since manager parts like to run the show, it can be tricky to distinguish them from your core self. To differentiate the manager, compare their emotions and actions to the list of core-self qualities I shared earlier in this chapter. Take an honest accounting.

Manager parts are the key to functional anxiety. Their qualities can actually be quite helpful for day-to-day functioning and lead to lots of success in life. But make sure their qualities are balanced and channeled in healthy ways. For example, let's say you are in charge of a business, leading seventy employees. When you were younger, you learned that successful people never let anything get in their way. So your manager part has an incredible work ethic, getting by on very little sleep to provide for the multi-faceted needs of your staff. As you get older, your body starts to tell you it can't survive with that kind of neglect anymore. Maybe it shuts down, with a low immune system or you develop autoimmune disorders. Because your manager part does not have boundaries and runs like a machine, your core self must take back the driver's seat quickly. Your core self needs to nurture this Energizer Bunny manager, and any wounded-child parts they may be protecting, into a more realistic role so you don't develop even more problems.

Manager parts are used to being in control, think in black and white, and don't like change—so there will be pushback. If managers feel bullied out of a role, unvalued, or criticized, they will return and redouble efforts to protect the status quo or an exiled part who is vulnerable and has something to prove. Other parts will likely flare up, raising their voices to help the manager protect its role. Through EMDR-style activities, you can learn to reparent parts like this that help you, but also hurt you. Other managers, like "the perfectionist," "the organizer," or "the one who perseveres" can also be both helpful and hurtful. To truly heal, manager parts must feel confident enough in the core self's ability to keep the exiled parts safe that they realize they don't need to step in. Manager parts need help realizing that they will not stop being valuable just because they slow down and try new ways. Your core self needs to kindly teach them how to be more balanced.

Do you recognize any qualities of the manager parts when you are triggered? What preventative and protective measures do you tend to apply? Think of some adaptive ways you've evolved over the years that can help your responses be more balanced.

Exercise: Getting to Know Your Parts

Think about a specific time when you felt triggered or overwhelmed. We all have many things we are actively worried about. Pull up the most relevant item from your laundry list of concerns. Call to mind the details to evoke some visceral reactions inside you. You will likely notice all sorts of things going on in your mind and body. Noticing what is going on inside can be overwhelming at first. Try to zero in on a quality that has both positive and destructive aspects to it, with the potential to both help you and hurt you.

On a single page, write the following details about this part. Use a different page for each subsequent part that you identify.

1. What is the main characteristic of the part?

2. Name the part. Names can be something descriptive, like Mr. Know-It-All, Ms. Busy Body, Doomy Gloomy, or Clean-up Crew.

3. How old does this part seem?

4. When you think about the part, what body sensations come up?

5. Where do you feel the sensations in your body?

6. What are some thoughts that come up as you think about the part?

7. Name some emotions the part is feeling.

8. What does this part look like?

9. List some of the part's core qualities.

10. Based on these core qualities, do you think this is an exile, a first responder, or a manager?

11. Which level of Erikson's model of psychosocial development do you think this part may be frozen at?

12. Based on this part's development, what do you think their unmet needs are?

13. How can you help this part feel that their needs are being met?

14. Try drawing a picture or finding an image that best represents this part. You may have a photo of yourself at that age. If this part reminds you of someone else, you can use a photo of them. You can also choose an emoji, animal, cartoon character, or any image that comes to mind when you think about this part.

Here is an example of one of Andrea's parts.

1. Main characteristic: Anxious

2. Name: The Chips Monster

3. Age: Eleven years old

4. Felt sense, or body sensations: Stomach grumbling, pit in throat, dry mouth, weak, jittery, unsettled, empty, skull tightening

5. Location in body: Head, throat, stomach

6. Thoughts that come up: I feel really bad for this part. She feels like she needs to hide and cover up who she is. She feels judged and has a lot to prove, but doesn't think she will ever be good enough. Nobody sees her for who she is. She puts on a show that everything is okay and binge eats in private. She is an overachiever to the outside world.

7. Emotions the part is feeling: Shame, pity, disgust, sad, lonely

8. Physical appearance: A mix of me when I was little, probably pudgier than I actually was, and she has my mother's face.

9. Core qualities: Impulsive, fearful, prone to all types of addictions, negative tone of voice, unpredictable, toxic positivity, sleeps too much or not enough, extreme dieting or overeating as a form of control, extreme obsessions with exercising, fixer, obsessive

10. Type of part (exile, first responder, manager): She is a first responder who gets into conflict with the manager a lot, in order to protect some younger exiled part.

11. Level of Erikson's psychosocial development: Very likely she's frozen at Stage 4 with insecurity, incompetency, and self-doubt. But she's protecting a much younger part dealing with autonomy, probably a Stage 2 young toddler who isn't allowed to make choices on their own.

12. Unmet needs: Autonomy, unconditional love, acceptance

13. How to help this part feel these needs are met: First, I have to strengthen my self-energy, building the confidence to help her believe that she is seen and understood. She needs to feel valued for the work she has done to keep the younger, more vulnerable part protected for so many years. Nobody can touch her with me in the driver's seat. She can feel protected and loved. I have to gain permission for this part to let go and let me now support the younger part. She needs to be convinced that my core self is strong enough to support the younger part. Then she can start to relax, maybe taking a beach vacation in my imagination.

As you work with each part like this, you may notice the part slowly maturing. The age, qualities, appearance, and associated sensations can change, evolving as you work with the individual part. That's normal! Just notice it and keep notes at the bottom of each page as the part morphs. Repeat this activity for other parts until you have a collection of pages, sort of like a catalog of your parts that you can refer to as you do EMDR-style work.

Fully engage this activity to the best of your ability, as many times as you need to. Get to know all your parts. Your goal is not to change anything or any part, but to remain curious. Curiosity is one of my favorite qualities of the core self. It helps us learn and grow and evolve through our lives. Now hold on to that curiosity as you learn the nuts and bolts of EMDR in the next chapter.

Chapter 7

Tools for Your EMDR Journey

Our goal with EMDR is not to make anxiety disappear entirely, but rather to befriend it, get to know it, and validate it. This ultimately reduces the hold anxiety has on us, as well as its intensity and frequency. When we become familiar with our anxious parts, we can learn how to support them better. As you set out to lead yourself through EMDR-style exercises, ensure you're not expecting to completely eliminate anxiety. The anxious parts of you offer some of the many defense mechanisms that have helped your ancestors survive scary situations throughout history. They formed to protect you when you needed them most. As I shared in chapter 1, this is a natural part of being human.

EMDR is known for its profound ability to bring about deep, positive, lasting change. The method was created by one of my heroes, Francine Shapiro, who inadvertently struck gold with her findings. She originally designed EMDR to help clients overcome posttraumatic stress disorder (PTSD), but over time, the therapy world realized that she had tapped into something significant and powerful—beyond healing big T trauma. Since trauma and stress impact the brain and body similarly, it makes sense that this tool works wonders for anxiety as well.

EMDR can help you get unstuck when your mind ruminates and your anxious behaviors start to wreak havoc in your life. It works well in tandem with other proven-effective therapies for anxiety, like classic cognitive behavioral therapy (CBT) and dialectical behavior therapy (DBT), as well as more body-based, somatic techniques. Successful outcomes can rely heavily on a therapist who creatively uses and integrates a variety of techniques at the same time. This chapter will teach you the signature features of EMDR. In the five phases that follow, I will guide you to draw on other therapeutic approaches as well. It all starts with scheduling time to do the exercises.

Set Aside Specific Time

Allocating specific time to do this work is essential. Not only does it ensure you will make progress, but the simple act of scheduling stimulates your brain's executive functions, which often get shut off when you're triggered. The stronger you can make this part of our brain, the more automatic the healing process will become. So take a moment to think about how much time you're willing to devote each week, ensure this is realistic, and mark it in your calendar.

Treat your time for EMDR as sacred time. You're tapping into your inner world. If your brain isn't there yet, read ahead and then come back to schedule time in a week or a month when you're feeling less scattered. Sometimes having a committed buddy to work with can make all the difference, like a gym buddy. If you have a friend or partner who would also be interested in taking their own self-led journey alongside you, set a weekly date to meet up and work together. Or call them after a session to share personal experiences.

The Process of EMDR

Here is a high-level summary of the processes involved in EMDR. As you learned in previous chapters, memories have a felt sense and emotions associated with them. They tend to get trapped inside our unconscious mind and our body, causing all sorts of anxiety symptoms. Their qualities are determined by the unmet needs we had during a particular stage of psychosocial development, or by significantly stressful events in later years.

In the upcoming phases, you will encounter the following processes that work together to alleviate anxiety symptoms and process specific anxieties. You will learn to:

- Identify *target memories* that you want to process

- Create a healing game plan through self-evaluations that assess those memories and associated feelings, beliefs, and body sensations

- Desensitize your nervous system by resetting the sensitivity levels of your internal alarms in order to process target memories

- Self-monitor and track progress

- Solidify your achievements with psychoeducation and a variety of integrative therapy tools

- Replace negative beliefs and maladaptive behaviors with more adaptive, healthier ones

- Process remaining physiological symptoms

- Strengthen self-energy, resilience, and emotional health by becoming more attuned to your felt sense and the many parts that form your inner world

- Practice mindfulness, grounding exercises, and body-scan techniques to support post-healing growth

In order to achieve success in a self-paced model, I provide you with a process that should be easier to do while working independently. Every day, you face unique challenges and struggles that fan the flames of latent anxiety. Maybe you are experiencing conflicts at work, are overwhelmed by what you see in the news, have difficulties with friends or family, struggle in school, or even fight battles within yourself over feeling not good enough or lost. As you face these challenges, anxiety can pop up in the background. I encourage you to think of this anxiety like a bright red, flashing light, signaling that something is not quite right. It is a sign that you can bring the experience into your EMDR journey.

The Challenge of Time Traveling

One of the fascinating, and sometimes confusing, traits of our brain is its natural ability to time travel. This journey through time can unexpectedly take us back to the past, replaying memories or experiences that are emotional or distressing. It could also catapult us into the future, a realm filled with what ifs, worst-case scenarios, uncertainty, and worry about things that haven't happened yet. Mental time travel can happen at the most inopportune times. It can mess with our inner peace and balance—especially when we find ourselves mentally somewhere else, unable to remember how we got there. Time travel can cause our body to react in the same way it would if we were really in that situation. Our thoughts are enough to catapult us into a state of autopilot emergency reactions, where we think, feel, and act in ways that aren't helpful.

There are times when visiting the past and envisioning the future are helpful. But for the most part, we aim to live in the present moment. When we do time travel, we want to do it intentionally, from a calm state. We want to be rational, fully led by our core self. EMDR is the vehicle that allows us to time travel in a structured way. The goal is to learn how to kindly guide our wandering mind back to the present moment, so we can deal with any concerns in a calm, logical way.

After your brain time travels, to reregulate or to get back to a balanced state, a range of techniques can come in handy. First off, realizing that you have traveled out of the present moment is an important step. Being aware that your mind has slipped into the past or the future is the first move to regain control. In chapter 1, you learned to put anxieties into a container with the containment exercise. In chapter 4, you learned that focusing on your felt sense can bring you back to the here and now. There are many more tools you can learn that help you break free of, recover from, and heal unwanted time travel. Some are included in this chapter and more can be found toward the end of the book. Others can be picked up along your life journey, as you live fully and face bumps head on.

There's No Place Like Home

As you embark on self-led EMDR, you might begin to time travel in a way that stimulates the alarm bells inside you. But time traveling in your mind isn't only about ruminating on past incidents or worrying about the future. We often create scenarios in our heads that are not grounded in truth at all. Our mind tends to create alternate realities too. In nearly the whole movie *The Wizard of Oz*, Dorothy was time traveling in her mind. Remember Dorothy's mantra "There's no place like home"? That saying helped her come back to reality, to home, in the end. It even helped her appreciate what she had taken for granted before. Like Dorothy, you may feel differently about your life after doing this work. If you feel discombobulated or out of sorts at any point, do some grounding and reorienting to remind yourself that you are safe, in the present moment, and everything is okay. In chapter 10, you will find more information about grounding and reorienting. For now, here are some ways to do it.

Exercise: Sensory Awareness Grounding

- With your eyes open, observe your surroundings, noticing as many details as you can for two minutes.

- Squeeze a squishy ball. Hug a pillow tightly or push it as hard as you can. Hold an ice-cold drink. Stroke a pet's fur. Do any of these things while focusing on the sensory experience and any shifts that happen in your body.

- Listen to soft, soothing music with your eyes closed and feet firmly on the ground. Notice shifts in your body as you let yourself relax into the sounds and vibrations. Become curious about how the music impacts your body sensations.

Exercise: Cognitive Awareness Reorientation

After an intense EMDR session, it's normal to feel a bit spacey, like you just woke up from a deep sleep. It's important to take a moment to *reorient* yourself in place and time. Ask yourself a few questions to help ground you.

1.   Where am I right now?

2.   What's the date today?

3.   How old am I?

Expanded anchoring statements include similar details, but also add things like your name, where you live, what time it is, and what tasks are on your agenda for the day. Here's a typical anchoring statement for me.

Today is Monday, May 3rd. It's 11:15 a.m. and I'm sitting at my desk enjoying my second warm, steaming cup of coffee. I have a client coming to my office in fifteen minutes. My heart is beating quickly as I collect my notes and prepare for the next client, so I'm taking some quiet time before the meeting starts. I will continue to do grounding and reorienting techniques to settle my nerves.

You can add even more details of sensations, if you'd like.

It was raining when I came to work this morning, but the sun is coming out. After my next client, I'll walk for fifteen minutes to breathe fresh air and touch dewy leaves on the birch trees. My coffee is warm to touch and feels sweetly bold inside my mouth, burning in a good way as I swallow it.

With these tools, you can manage your state as you move in and out of EMDR exercises. They can also help throughout your day as you navigate stressors and stimulations. You always want to return home, to the present moment and your felt sense of being here.

Assess Your Distress Level

You'll want to check in with how you're feeling before, during, and after each session. The subjective units of distress scale (SUDS) is like a thermometer for your emotions. It helps you track how intense your feelings are at any given moment, so you can see how they change as you work through your target memories. Start by rating your distress from 0 (completely relaxed) to 10 (extremely distressed), and use this scale to monitor your progress over time.

10: Extremely distressed, overwhelmed

 9: Very distressed, hard to focus

 8: Very uncomfortable, tough to manage

 7: Pretty distressed, feeling off balance

 6: Moderate distress, still functional

 5: Average distress, managing okay

 4: Mild distress, still able to function

 3: Minimal distress, easy to manage

 2: Barely any distress, comfortable

 1: Calm, alert, clear

 0: Fully relaxed, at peace

When you first start thinking about difficult memories, it's totally normal for the distress level to be high. The goal is for that number to gradually go down as you work through the EMDR process. When you reach a 3 or 4, you should feel more settled.

If the distress level starts rising instead of dropping, it's okay to pause and do a grounding exercise. Remember, this is a process, so taking breaks along the way is part of honoring your needs. With practice, you'll become more skilled at managing your emotions through this journey. Be patient with yourself—you're doing important work.

Rewiring Your Brain with Bilateral Stimulation

Very gentle rhythms can help settle our mind, allowing us to relax the parts of our brain that tends to think too much. This rhythmic stimulus also activates the deeper parts of the brain that stores our memories. The signature feature of EMDR is a back-and-forth movement called *bilateral stimulation.* There are a variety of ways to achieve this meditative therapeutic rhythm, even though the name EMDR indicates that eye movement is involved. Research has found that any type of bilateral stimulation could be effective, not just following back-and-forth movements with your eyes. It can work using electronic stimulus or a tapping rhythm. This EMDR journey will use tapping to uncover sensations and emotions tied to your memories, and reprocess them in ways that open a clear path for healing and growth. Essentially, the bilateral stimulation of tapping helps rewire your brain in a more organized, healthy way. Then it works to build new, stronger neural pathways.

Exercise: The Butterfly Hug

The Butterfly Hug is the technique you'll use in your self-led sessions for bilateral stimulation. It was created by a brilliant person named Lucina Artigas. Instead of using physical touch, buzzers, or other in-person strategies, the butterfly hug allows you to do bilateral stimulation on your own. Plus, you get a nice, warm, fuzzy self-hug in the process. Here's how it works:

1. Cross your arms over your chest like you're giving yourself a hug.

2. Tap your upper arms, one after the other, in a slow and steady left-right, left-right rhythm.

3. Continue this steady beat throughout each session.

Try this for a minute or two right now, before moving on. Keep up the tapping rhythm until you feel like some tension has released from your body. The more you practice, the better you'll get. Set a time each day to practice the left-right tapping rhythm. I recommend practicing at night, right before bed for two minutes. It can be very soothing and may help you sleep better. That said, if you find tapping stimulating, and this rhythm has the opposite effect, try it first thing in the morning or after lunch. Consistency is what matters most. Pick a time when you know you'll have two to five uninterrupted minutes, and set an alarm on your phone to remind you to do it daily.

At the reprocessing stage, you may find it challenging to stay aware of two things at the same time—the tapping rhythm and how you feel inside. It can take a little while to get the hang of it, so don't be discouraged if it feels tough at first and be sure to practice ahead.

When you are working with target memories, this tapping will help you feel calmer. It will loosen up any of the pent-up stress you're feeling. I'll provide some scripts to help guide you through sessions during the upcoming phases. For now, you can try this practice script as you do the butterfly hug.

Exercise: Butterfly Hug with a Script

Doing the butterfly hug while following a script might feel a bit strange at the beginning but keep trying. With practice, it'll feel more natural and holding dual awareness will become easier. This is a technique you can use any time you need to calm down and ground yourself. The following script doesn't ask you to dive into any memories, so it's a safe way to start practicing for the real deal. As you do the butterfly tapping, follow this script.

Breathe slowly and deeply from deep inside your belly. Observe what is going on in your mind and body—your thoughts, sensations, emotions—just observe what's going on, without trying to change anything. Don't try to push your thoughts away or judge them. Notice any movements or shifts inside. Notice any sensations that are happening. Sit with it all. Just notice the presence of any thoughts, feelings, and sensations.

You can use this tool like a first-aid kit for those moments when you're not feeling settled and can't figure out why.

Preparing for the EMDR Phases

The traditional model of EMDR uses eight phases (Shapiro 1995). I have worked to simplify this process for you and adapted the original eight-phase structure into a five-phase model that's more conducive to independent work. If you want to learn more about the eight phases, I suggest visiting the EMDR training website at https://www.emdria.org/blog/the-eight-phases-of-emdr-therapy/. It offers a concise overview of each phase and how EMDR would work with a therapist. You will be attempting to achieve similar results on your own, but obviously, the process is not the same as it would be working with a therapist.

I highly recommend that you read through all the following phases first, to gain a thorough overview of what you'll be doing. Then return to Phase 1 and start doing the practices. I know it may feel like a lot to take in when you read through the phases. If you feel overwhelmed by the enormity of the process, you can pat yourself on the back and congratulate yourself on being totally human. It is a lot of work to untangle the strands of what's been keeping you stuck. But it's not insurmountable when you commit to the process and take baby steps. While being anxious would be normal, I hope that all the preparation work you have done has you pumped and ready to jump into our first phase! Join me when you're ready.

Part Three

The EMDR Journey Through Panic, Fear, Stress, and Worry

Getting to Know Yourself Better

A big part of EMDR is about reorganizing the way our brain works. It's like cleaning out and organizing a "stuff drawer." We all have that one chaotic drawer or closet in our house where we stash things out of sight—until it becomes so full we can't shove one more paper clip into it. Similarly, when our nervous system is reaching maximum capacity, anxiety happens. Our autopilot responses spill out all over the place. Doing EMDR is like cleaning up and reorganizing this "stuff drawer" in our brain, chucking out the clutter, putting back things you want in a more efficient way, and fixing broken items that you value. At first, this can feel overwhelming, and it's normal for things to look a bit messier before they start looking better.

If you haven't started using a journal yet, I highly suggest you start now. This way, you can organize and reorganize everything that comes up during your EMDR journey. You can start a binder with a mix of blank and lined paper, dividers or folders with pockets for cue cards, and sheet protectors. Be flexible, let your creativity flow, and have fun with creating your personal record. Embrace the journey!

In therapy, intakes are "getting to know you" sessions. Because you want to make real change and build a strong foundation for your overall well-being, get to know yourself better. Recording how you got to where you are and learning more about your inner family of parts will help focus your EMDR work. We'll start your self-intake with the people in your life.

Identify Your Rings of Connection

Let's clarify the people in your life and how close they are to you. In your journal, draw a dartboard with your name in the bullseye. Each ring of the dartboard represents different groupings of people in your life.

1. The rings near the center are your closest connections, the people who mean the most to you. Be very discerning. There should be three to five people who *really* matter.

2. In the ring after that, write the names of family members, friends, and people who have greatly influenced your life.

3. As you get farther away from your inner circle, keep adding rings for different levels of acquaintances.

Your garbage man is important because if he wasn't in your life, your house would stink. But he is not close to being as significant as your teacher from preschool who gave you the confidence to read out loud. Including people like the garbage man might be a bit excessive.

You can include people who had a negative impact on your life as well. This is optional. If you do choose to include them, you may find that those who made the greatest impact on your life are the same people who have also hurt you. Any people in your life who made a significant impression on you, whether positive or negative, can all find a place on this dartboard. If you're unsure whether to include someone, think of your earliest memory of them. Did they make an impact on your thoughts, feelings, or actions? If yes, include them. If unsure, include them anyway.

Describe the People in Your Life

Now, turn to the next page in your binder and dive a little deeper. You are going to write details about each person. You might find it helpful to use a different page for each person, with lots of room to add notes about them as memories pop up. Start with the inner circle you drew on the previous page and work your way outward, section by section.

In this activity, you will answer specific questions about these people. Feel free to scribble down as much as you want for each question. Don't worry if you can't think of specific details right away, you can always add more information later. Feel free to decorate the pages and add pictures or artifacts.

Write the first person's name at the top of the page. Then add details about them, like:

- How they are related or connected to you.

- Their birthday (if you know it).

- The age you were when they came into your life.

Create a brief description of the person, with details like these.

- Where they live, or used to live.

- Whether or not you knew them personally. This may seem strange, but you may feel a strong connection with people you've never met, like a deceased sibling, estranged grandparent, or pop-culture hero.

- How long you've known them.

- How you relate to them. Do you get highly triggered by them? Do they give you warm-fuzzy feelings? Maybe they inspire you, as a mentor.

Then, for each person, write about your experience of them.

- Your earliest memories of them, including your age at the time and any other details that might be important.

- Your most significant memories of them.

- Whether those memories or your feelings toward them have shifted over time. How?

- Any phrases, adjectives, and emotions that come to mind when you think of them. It's normal to have seemingly conflicting emotions about a single person. One person

can represent goodness and kindness, and also be triggering to you in some ways. Relationships are complicated.

- Any felt-sense sensations you experience when you think
  of them.

- If you are triggered by them, how old do you feel when you
  think of them or when you think of responding to them?
  For example, you could feel vulnerable and emotional, like
  a three- or four-year-old. Or stubborn and rebellious like a
  teenager.

- Write down anything about their past that might influence
  the way they treat you. Perhaps they were refugees, immi-
  grants, went through a war, or had a major accident. Were
  they abandoned? Orphaned? Did they have complicated
  relationships with their parents or siblings? Did they lose a
  loved one early in life?

If you have a good relationship with someone now, you may want
to ask them to share stories with you. We can carry perceptions and
emotional baggage that are not our own, and they may help trace
something back to someone else's story. Then you can let go of it more
easily during EMDR processing.

Look back at the parts of yourself that you identified in chapter 3.
See whether any of them look or sound like one of the people you have
identified. Perhaps you inherited an autonomic response from one of
them? You might also notice that some of your parts come to the
surface when you interact with certain people (like a stubborn teen
part who tends to snap back at a parent). Do you have any early memories linking one of your parts to this person? Don't feel bad if this is
confusing. You can skip it for now and try again after you have done
more work with your parts.

Journal About Your Experience

Treat your journal as your therapist or confidant. Establishing a personal relationship with your journal will hopefully offer the sense of

connection you need to work through some of the tough stuff on your own. Here are some prompts to get you started.

Describe your closest relationships: Who do you feel closest to now? These will probably be the people you listed closest to the center of your dartboard. What makes these relationships important? Write about any significant shifts in each relationship over time. Do you have any visceral reactions when you think of them? Do they make you feel comfortable in your skin, or is it complicated?

Childhood reactions: As a child, how did you tend to react when you got upset? Did you have any self-talk messages, or things other people said, that made you feel better or worse? Perhaps these used to motivate you, but now they make you feel low or inadequate or shamed, like "Suck it up," "Be a man," or "Big girls don't cry." Do you find yourself behaving similarly now? Write about whether you use these shaming tactics to try to motivate yourself now.

Triggers: Are you regularly triggered by similar incidents or types of people? For example, around certain types of people you tend to be overly argumentative. Perhaps you find yourself lying whenever you feel someone is being confrontational. Or you get really agitated if people are late. Maybe when you hear kids screaming, your heart starts racing and your back starts hurting. Pick your earliest memory of reacting similarly or in a way that feels connected somehow. Let's say you recall being around five years old, watching your brothers fighting and screaming at each other. Your mother came downstairs and screamed so loud her face contorted into a monster-like scowl. It scared you to your core. Your heart was racing and a chill shot down your spine. Later on, you may think of even earlier associations, so be ready to revisit this entry. For now, just write whatever comes to mind. Try to figure out who in your life feels the most associated with these triggers. How do you react to them now? How did you react when you were younger?

Earliest Mentors: When you were younger, who was your go-to person for advice? Can you remember some good advice that stuck with you? Can you remember any that turned out to be horrible advice? Who do you turn to for advice or mentoring now? Does their guidance make you feel better or worse?

Caregiver Attachment: What's your earliest memory of being away from your parents? Describe the story in as much detail as you can. How old were you? How did you feel about it?

Early Struggles: Can you remember feeling rejected, misunderstood, or abandoned as a child? Jot down some stories, memories, and details. How do these early experiences still affect you now?

There is a lot to unpack in each of these prompts, so you might break it down even further. Each prompt could be three to five (or more) journal entries. You can also spread this out over time, if you need to. You could be itching to jump to the next part by now. That's understandable. Just make a date with yourself so you have a set time to come back to these journaling prompts.

Identify Target Memories

We all have memories of events or experiences that cause us continuing distress and contribute to anxiety. In an EMDR session, we call these *target memories* to mind in order to reprocess them, so our brain can find a new way to relate to them that reduces the memory's impact. You can prepare to do this by sorting out the most relevant information from your life, in order to identify these target memories. This helps us focus and prepare for when we will begin processing our target memories in Phase 2: Unpacking the Past.

A helpful framework for working with memories is a tool called TIPCES: Target, Image, Part, Cognition, Emotion, and Sensation. This structure was created by EMDR founder Francine Shapiro. I've added the P to connect our work with parts, which you explored in chapters 5 and 6. Think of TIPCES as your guide through this process. You can download a template at http://www.integrativepsych.co/emdrforanxiety.

Start by looking through your self-intake notes and identifying patterns or memories that stand out—moments that still trigger you, or any recurring issues that impact you deeply. Write down one memory or theme per page. These will become the target memories you will focus on in your self-led EMDR sessions. For each of these memories, use the TIPCES structure to break them down.

Trigger: Describe the specific event or situation that caused you to feel anxious or stressed. (Such as a harsh comment from your boss or a family argument.)

Image: Picture the scene as vividly as you can, like a snapshot or a movie. Write down the details: sounds, sights, smells, and how it all felt.

Parts: Reflect on the parts of you who seem most connected to this memory. Is there a protective part stepping in, or maybe an exiled child part? It's okay if you're not sure, just write down what feels right for now.

Cognition: This is an exploration of your beliefs. What did this memory make you believe about yourself? (Such as, *I'm not good enough* or *I'm not safe*.) Write these down. Rate how strongly you believe that thought, on a scale from 1 (you don't believe it at all) to 7 (you believe it completely). Then try to identify a desired positive belief that will better serve you, like *I am enough just as I am*. We'll dive deeper into these core beliefs in Phase 2. You can always come back to this section once we explore your core beliefs further.

Emotions: List the emotions you felt during the event (like fear, anger, or sadness). If you have trouble pinpointing exactly how you felt, try searching for a list of emotions online that you can use to clarify your own feelings at the time.

Sensations: During the anxious or stressful event, physical sensations likely came up. Was your heart racing? Did you feel tension in your body? Write down where you felt sensations in your body. Then rate your distress level using the SUDS scale you learned earlier in this chapter.

Here's an example of a completed TIPCES log.

Target Memory: I felt embarrassed at work and have been avoiding my boss ever since.

Trigger: My boss criticized my work in front of a group of colleagues. It wasn't the first time, but it was the breaking point.

Image: I was at the meeting, already anxious. My boss walked in with his fancy tie and latte, making me feel small. I was asked to present, and he shouted at me to speak louder. My face turned red, my heart raced, and I ran to my office, feeling humiliated.

Part: An anxious part, probably protected by a few other parts. I'll revisit this after processing.

Cognition: My negative core belief is, *I'm not good enough.* My belief rating, before processing, is a 7. The positive belief that I desire is, *I am enough just as I am.*

Emotions: I feel embarrassed, anxious, helpless, frustrated.

Sensations: I experience sweaty palms, tightness in my chest, a knot in my stomach, and my heart pounding.

Take your time filling out a TIPCES log for each memory. Don't rush through it. If you're eager to begin processing right away, I suggest you start with the memory that feels most relevant right now. You can always return to the rest of your logs later, after your first processing round.

Organize Your Memories into Clusters

Once you've completed your TIPCES logs, you're ready to organize your memories into clusters. This helps you decide the order in which you will process them. You can group your memories by theme, emotion, or impact—whatever feels right. You can even use cue cards for this part, jotting down each target memory on a separate card and organizing them later. This way, you can start processing the most pressing memories while keeping the others ready for later.

Organizing your memories helps calm the mind, but remember, there's no rush. The goal is progress, not perfection. Take your time and trust the process. You'll come back to your memory clusters when you're ready to continue. This is another effective way to shelf some of the things you are currently anxious about, so you can deal with them later (like you did in the containment exercise in chapter 1). Here are some ideas for how you can organize your target memories into clusters. The order you follow to process your memories is totally up to you.

Most Bothersome: Look through your self-intake and find the memories or current issues that cause your stomach to wrench, your heart rate to increase, or your anxieties to flare up the most. These are things you tend to ruminate about or that haunt you most deeply.

Most Often: As you skim through your self-intake, see if any words or phrases keep popping up. For example, you may see the word "betrayed" a lot or maybe "lonely." Group all of those target memories with similar themes together. Continue grouping recurring themes together in clusters, like you would sort puzzle pieces by colors, patterns, and edge pieces.

Most Recent: Group the issues that have been coming up recently. Perhaps you feel bossed around by your brother a lot lately. Or you feel completely underappreciated at work. These issues can be anything that has been triggering your anxiety lately. Then order your target memories in chronological order, from newest to oldest.

Most Significant: Identify memories that have the most emotional weight or seem to drive a lot of unhealthy patterns. These are the ones causing the most anxiety or distress in your day-to-day life.

Don't worry about getting every detail right just yet. You can always revisit and add new memories later. We'll explore each one more deeply in the next phase. It's helpful to make sure you have the right tools to guide you through the self-led EMDR process. Checking in with yourself regularly helps set you up for success. TIPCES isn't just useful for past memories—it's also a great way to track new issues as they arise. If something is bothering you in your current life, like a recent conflict with someone close to you, write it down in a TIPCES log. Even if the event isn't tied to an old memory, organizing your thoughts can help you process and understand your feelings better.

Now that you have packed your bags with basic EMDR tools, you can embark on this journey toward self-discovery and heightened emotional health. As you travel through all the phases of EMDR, you will make a lot of new friends. Your parts are waiting for you to get to know them better! And you will find lots of buried treasures inside that you never knew existed. Let's apply all you have learned to reprocessing your past.

Unpacking the Past

Venturing into your past can feel like entering a wilderness. These terrains, packed with memories and experiences, have played major roles in shaping who you are today. During your self-intake in the last phase, you unpacking these memories methodically. This a big part of the journey toward understanding yourself better, so you can heal and grow.

In this chapter, we're going to work with your memory clusters and find out as much as we can about the roots of each one. As we do this, some roadblocks may arise, because dealing with the past has the potential to feel challenging. Remember to stay in your zone of tolerance while also recognizing that, no matter how tough this journey might seem, it can be a stepping stone toward a healthier state of mind, a stronger self, and a happier life. As we start working with core beliefs, it's important to see negative thoughts clearly.

Negative Thoughts Based on Past Experience

Our core beliefs are the deeply ingrained ideas we hold about ourselves, others, and the world—often shaped by past experiences. These beliefs act like lenses, coloring how we see things. Sometimes these lenses can distort reality. This means that our perceptions aren't always a true reflection of what's really going on.

Core beliefs can sometimes hold us back, causing us to fall into patterns of self-doubt or unhealthy thinking. But the beautiful thing is, *we have the power to change them.* By becoming more aware of where our thoughts come from, we can begin to replace the limiting beliefs with ones that are kinder, more realistic, and empowering.

As you navigate this journey of self-discovery, pay attention to any negative or self-critical thoughts that arise. These often point to a deeper belief that might need some gentle reevaluation. Psychiatrist Aaron T. Beck, who pioneered cognitive behavior therapy (CBT), emphasized that recognizing these patterns—called *cognitive distortions*—can help us shift our mindset. When you notice these negative thoughts, here are some compassionate questions to ask yourself. They can help uncover any beliefs that may no longer serve you.

- **Am I thinking in all-or-nothing terms?** Does everything feel like a win or a loss, with nothing in between?

- **Am I overgeneralizing?** If something didn't go well once, does that mean it will never go right again?

- **Am I assuming failure before even trying?** Remember, the only real way to fail is not to try at all.

- **Am I focusing only on the negative?** When I get one piece of criticism, do I forget all the positive things people said?

- **Am I jumping to conclusions?** Do I worry about what will happen next without real evidence?

- **Am I dismissing my strengths?** Do I find it hard to recognize what I do well, or feel unappreciated?

- **Am I assuming I can read others' minds?** Am I making guesses about their intentions when I don't know for sure?

- **Am I magnifying or minimizing things?** Do I blow up small issues or downplay important ones?

- **Am I open to being wrong?** Can I listen to others' points of view, knowing I might learn something new?

- **Am I stuck in "should haves" or "could haves"?** Am I blaming myself for things that happened outside of my control?

Did any of those scenarios feel familiar? When these types of cognitive distortions run through your head, it's a sign that your wounded-child and protective parts are trying to reinforce their deeply rooted, harmful core beliefs. The cognitive distortions behind the core beliefs we identify offer a surefire way to recognize their source—the misguided voices of your parts rather than your wise and compassionate self.

Remember, this process isn't about perfection—it's about being kind to yourself and gently shifting your perspective over time. *You deserve to see yourself through a more compassionate lens,* one that reflects your strengths and growth, not just your limitations. With each new insight, you're creating space for healthier, more balanced beliefs that help you step into your fullest potential.

Misguided Core Beliefs That Continue to Harm You

Your core beliefs about yourself and others can become self-fulfilling prophecies if you don't learn how to adjust them. It's like wearing glasses with the wrong prescription. Everything seems blurry and distorted, but we get used to seeing the world in that way and can't imagine it being different. We come to think these thoughts are normal and true. But you have the power to shift your beliefs and see the world in a brighter, clearer way. The key is shifting toward more self-compassionate, creative, patient beliefs.

If you are not used to being validating and compassionate with yourself, this will change the way you talk to and think about yourself in significant ways. For example, it is unhelpful to tell a part that's feeling stupid, "Stop feeling stupid!" or "Stop being frustrated!" This just reinforces the part's distorted beliefs and deepens its feelings of being unloved and misunderstood. While our unhelpful (and sometimes destructive) core beliefs have hundreds of nuances, we can generally group them into common themes. Judith Beck (2005, 2011) narrowed it down to three categories: helplessness, belonging, and worthiness. Two more categories are also helpful to address: safety and responsibility.

Let's look at examples of misguided core beliefs related to *worthiness* and also some ideas for potential ways parts can shift their cognitions a bit with some positivity.

Misguided Core Belief	Healthier Belief
I am inherently bad.	*I am inherently good.*
I don't deserve anything good.	*I deserve goodness and kindness from the people I choose to associate with.*
I am worthless.	*I am inherently worthy even when I can't feel it.*
I'm defective.	*I was created just as I am meant to be, and I will continue to grow and evolve throughout my life like every other human.*
I'm flawed beyond repair.	*I am human, and humans make mistakes, but I am inherently good. I will continue to make mistakes because I am human too. That does not make me a flawed person.*
I'm stupid.	*I have specific things I am good at and know how to do. I will continue to learn and grow throughout my life.*
I don't matter.	*I matter to those who are worthy of my caring.*
I'm just a big failure.	*I am human, and I fail sometimes. I get knocked down and then get back up again. Each time I learn more.*

As you can see, to correct beliefs we aren't necessarily looking for *opposite* beliefs or untrue statements. We want the new beliefs to be accurate, hopeful, and validating. For example, if you are physically weak due to chronic illness, shifting the statement "I am weak" to "I am strong" is not truthful or helpful. A more helpful statement might be "I may be weaker in body, but I am determined to become stronger in spirit and make meaning in my life with whatever energy I have each day. I will try to have patience for my body and appreciate it when my body is able to do the things I really want to do." Now that you've looked at examples of how to shift the lens of some core beliefs related to worthiness, you can practice doing the same for the other categories.

Exercise: Shifting the Lens

Try shifting the lens yourself. Here is a simple, straightforward cognitive behavioral therapy (CBT) method you can use to help identify and change your core beliefs.

Step 1: In your journal, divide a page into two columns. In the first column, list unhelpful core beliefs that you believe to be "true." You can draw from the list that I will soon provide with examples related to helplessness and belonging, as well as the examples for worthiness I previously discussed—or come up with your own.

Step 2: Look at the first core belief on your list and consider whether it makes sense for you to maintain this belief. Ask yourself if you actually believe that it's true. Can you think of a good reason why you might feel the need to continue to hold onto it as truth? Is it protecting you in some way? Are there any advantages or disadvantages of continuing to believe it?

Step 3: Try to shift the lens to a more helpful statement. Remember, this may not be an opposite statement. Your helpful statement needs to be accurate for your situation and validate you. Sometimes positive affirmations can help shift the lens and support new core beliefs as they take root. There is a list of ideas for mantras you can use in chapter 10. It's normal if you need some help to inspire your new statements. It can feel challenging at first.

Step 4: Now try adjusting those lenses to see the world with a fresh perspective! If you still find it challenging, you can download a free mini e-book called "Anatomy of a Shame Spiral" at http://www.integrativepsych.co/emdrfor anxiety that can help you delve deeper into this work.

Here are some examples of the other categories of destructive core beliefs that you can add to your chart.

Helplessness	Belonging
I am trapped	Nobody wants me
I'm unsafe	I'm alone
I am doomed forever	I'm better off alone
I am a loser	Nobody understands me
I am weak	Nobody loves me
I always fail no matter what	Everybody hates me
I can't change	I don't need anybody else
This is just the way I am	I just don't fit in
I will never succeed	I don't belong anywhere
I can't	I don't belong in a relationship
I'm never the best	I am just unlovable
There is no point in trying	
Safety	**Responsibility**
I am unsafe	I must be perfect
The world is a dangerous place	I'm responsible for others' feelings
I cannot trust others	If something goes wrong, it's my fault
I have to always be on guard	
Bad things always happen to me	I have to take care of everything
I will never be protected	I can't rely on anyone else
My feelings are not valid	I should have done more
	It's my duty to fix everything

Connect Core Beliefs with Anxious Parts

As you explore your past and the reality of your formed belief system, you may see your anxious parts through kinder eyes, understanding that they came about because they were needed. These parts were your survival strategies, each one formed to deal with a specific situation or environment, looking out for you or filling an unmet need. The aim isn't to kick these parts out of the inner family, it is to help them find healthier, more helpful roles.

Look at your self-intake binder. Go through the parts pages and the TIPCES logs, then connect them with beliefs that they may be carrying. Here are some examples of parts and the core beliefs they might hold due to different life experiences. These ideas might help your parts adjust their misguided core beliefs.

Part Name: "The People-Pleaser"

Early Experience: Having to hide my true feelings to fit in

Misguided Core Belief: My feelings don't matter

Healthier Belief: My feelings are actually important

Part Name: "The Suppressor"

Early Experience: Being told to stop being a baby and that my emotions are annoying

Misguided Core Belief: My emotions are a burden

Healthier Belief: Emotions are a part of being human and all of them are welcome

Part Name: "The Martyr"

Early Experience: Being overly selfless in order to be liked

Misguided Core Belief: My own needs don't matter

Healthier Belief: My needs are important to me just as your needs are important to you, so let's see how we can get both of our needs met

Our ultimate goal in this book is to build a strong foundation of understanding, accepting, and kindness toward all your parts. As you untangle your past and get to know these parts, you're opening the door to healing and growth. The parts of your mind that used to protect you can become your guides on this journey to discover yourself and grow stronger.

Spot Triggers for Your Anxious Parts

Triggers are any words, situations, or even people that set off big emotional fireworks inside us or a flood of intense feelings and somatic sensations. Often, being triggered is like a knee-jerk reaction that comes out of the blue. Knowing our triggers gives us a window into our inner world of parts that we would not otherwise see. Spotting the triggers for our anxious parts isn't a simple game of "I spy"—it needs quiet thinking time, patience, and a lot of honesty with ourselves.

The first step when spotting triggers is simply noticing when you suddenly feel anxious, sad, angry, or upset without any heads up. When you feel a big, intense emotional change, it can be an opportune moment to stop and think about what happened *right before* that change. Was there a certain situation, comment, smell, place, or person that made you feel different? Sometimes, the trigger is sneaky and not directly linked to the feelings it brings up. For example, a certain song might make you feel sad because it reminds you of a tough time in childhood. But you know you are currently okay in reality. You may not even remember that, as a child, you had an intense emotional reaction to the song, but for some reason now it's bringing up big feelings. Keep track of these little details in your binder, as they show up. Then you can add any triggers you might be interested in exploring to your target memories list, so they're ready and waiting on cue for processing later.

Next, identify the anxious part associated with a trigger. This helps you understand why certain triggers set off emotional firecrackers inside. For instance, say you know that being around a certain type of person triggers a worried part because of past embarrassment. With this understanding, you can comfort this part, letting it know that although you couldn't keep it safe in the past, you've grown since then. Now, as an adult, you have tools to get through this type of challenge in a more helpful and adaptive way.

Figuring out triggers for your anxious parts is like an escape room or a mystery game. Each clue you find gives you a better understanding of yourself and the evolution of your personality. This expanding understanding and insight into your inner world will help you learn to manage your feelings and reactions better as you grow and mature with more confidence and control. Now that you have identified a list of target memories to process, let's explore how to unpack them.

Exercise: Processing Target Memories

As you learn the processing part of your journey, and get ready to unpack your first memory, be sure to read ahead—before applying this tool. You will be addressing each of your stuck parts of an unprocessed memory by helping the brain store information in newer and more helpful ways. When a memory is successfully processed, it will leave you feeling more settled, with increased clarity about the memory. I can't emphasize enough that we are not trying to get rid of a memory, a part, or an emotion. We are just trying to lessen the disturbance that the memory is causing inside. When the processing is done, you will find that the memory no longer causes as much disturbance in your day-to-day life. You will have less anxiety and stress from triggers that were unconsciously associated with those memories. Here are the steps to follow.

Preparation

1. Pull out your first TIPCES log associated with the first target memory you want to process. Read through what you have written.

2. Notice your felt sense and any other body sensations that comes up as you think of this target memory.

3. Notice your emotions as you think of this target memory. Reflect on more nuanced emotions that come up.

4. Looking at your TIPCES log again, think of the first time you ever felt similar sensations and emotions. How old were you? Who were you with? Do you have other memories or relationships that cause you to feel similarly?

Reprocessing

1. Recall ways this incident sprouted an unhelpful or untrue belief for you.

2. Just like we did a bit earlier in the chapter, figure out a new belief that is healthier and makes more sense to you given your new reality.

3. Consider what you want to achieve from processing this memory, perhaps how you ideally want to respond when triggered again.

4. Fill out your pre-session SUDS score. Always check on the intensity of your felt sense and emotions at the *beginning* and *end* of each reprocessing session. This way, you can track progress and decide if you need to do another round of processing.

Bilateral Stimulation

1. Using the Butterfly Hug technique you learned in chapter 7, start bilateral stimulation. Recall specific features of your target memory and all the surrounding experiences. Remember, you aren't trying to change your experience. You are just noticing, with curiosity and compassion, all the details you have gathered. Notice what you feel in your body, where you feel it, and any other felt sense experiences that come up. Notice the emotions and where you feel them in your body. Are they shifting? Changing? Are they morphing into something else? If they are disturbing you, breathe into the spot that feels uncomfortable and then blow all discomfort out. Continue to tap your shoulders in an alternating rhythm.

2. Keep tapping and think about the misguided core beliefs you have about yourself that are connected to this target memory. Stay with those ideas for a moment. Focus on the part of you associated with this belief and imagine validating and nurturing that part, giving it the love and support it always needed.

3. When you begin to feel a bit lighter, share more with this part. Tell them about your new, healthier belief that is now much truer than your old belief. Again, if you have any body sensations that are disturbing, imagine giving them space to travel inside you. Then then breathe them out.

4. Continue bilateral stimulation for a minimum of 30 more seconds.

Check In

1. Fill out your SUDS scale again. Hopefully you have decreased the intensity of your emotions by at least a few points.

2. Repeat steps 8 to 10 until you have a SUDS scale that's at 3 or below.

Depending on how complicated the memory you worked with is, you may want to take a break for a day or two. Then try reprocessing the same memory again followed by checking in through the SUDS scale another day.

Exercise: Grounding After a Session

Sometimes after a session you will feel out of sorts, tired, or spacey, like you just woke up from a deep sleep and are disoriented. When this happens, do a grounding or reorienting exercise to get you back to the present moment. Let's try a short one called 5, 4, 3, 2, 1 (Hendriksen 2018).

With your feet firmly on the ground and your back straight, take a deep breath in for 5 seconds, then out for 8 seconds. Do this two more times. Then let your breathing flow at a more natural pace as you become aware of your surroundings with all your senses. Notice what's around you in the following ways.

- Notice 5 things you see. For example: a spot on the floor, a decorative pillow, a picture on the wall...

- Notice 4 things you can touch. For example: a fuzzy blanket, a cold glass, grass under your feet...

- Notice 3 things you can hear. For example: birds chirping, a computer humming, your tummy grumbling...

- Notice 2 things you can smell. For example: the lotion you used on your hands, the woodsy smell of a piece of paper, your cup of coffee...

- Notice 1 thing you can taste. For example: the gum in your mouth, the drink sitting next to you, the protein bar you have in your purse...

You'll find more grounding exercises in chapter 8 that you can try. Use them after reprocessing sessions and whenever they feel helpful. After you're feeling a bit more grounded, go back and reflect on how the processing exercise was for you. However you feel it went, give yourself a pat on the back and a warm hug. It can take a lot out of you. If you need to, take a break from your processing work for a day or two (or even a week). Then whenever you feel ready, go through these same steps again, in another round, to process the next memory on your target list.

As you start doing rounds on this journey, processing different target memories, new insights might come up. More serious triggers could appear or you might even find that a memory on your list doesn't bother you at all anymore after working through others. Your initial plan can accommodate these possibilities as you adjust your target memory clusters and reorder them as needed.

This is a journey, not a race. You're not trying to win a gold medal for speed. You're more like a detective, investigating clues from your past without any preconceived judgment. Be patient, allow for shifts and changes, and understand that it's totally fine to modify your plan as you go along.

Oftentimes when we work intensely with our inner child parts and our anxious parts, we start to feel too connected to their emotional and sensory experiences. We need to differentiate ourselves from our parts and create a safe distance from raw memories. Here's an activity that can help.

Exercise: Differentiating Yourself from Anxious Parts

This powerful imagination exercise helps you create this distance by looking at your memories as if watching them on the big screen at a movie theater. It lets you observe what's going on for your parts, without getting too caught up in the intensity of their feelings and reactions.

Picture this: You're stepping into a movie theater to watch a special movie. It's the movie of your life. You find a comfy seat, the lights go down, and the movie starts. Each scene is a memory from your past. But you're not inside the movie, you're just sitting back to watch it from your comfy recliner seat.

Now, some scenes might be super intense, and you might feel a rush of strong emotions. But remember, you've got the remote control. If you need to, you can pause, step out of the theater, take a breather, rewind, fast forward, or close the curtains. Just like a scary movie can't really hurt you, these memories can't harm you in the here and now—even though they might be uncomfortable.

This isn't about pretending things didn't happen. Rather, it's a magic trick to turn down the dial on the intensity of emotional hurt. This can help you handle the memories in a more relaxed and thoughtful way. You can even try this visualization during your next round of EMDR as you do your bilateral stimulation and process a target memory.

Congratulations, you have learned how to guide yourself through an EMDR-style session! Give yourself a huge hug. I'm sure it wasn't easy to dive into your past, but hopefully you feel a sense of accomplishment. This process is here for you whenever you need it. Now that you can navigate processing past memories, you can learn how to live your most meaningful life—without succumbing to the chronic time travel that triggers anxiety and stress. Get ready to embrace the gift of the present moment.

Embracing the Present

Our world can feel unpredictable sometimes. Every day throws new puzzles, adventures, and curveballs at us, requiring us to constantly adjust. Often, our minds time travel between the past and the future, while the present—the real deal—quietly passes by, like an unnoticed treasure. The present moment, what we call "the here and now," is packed with magic. It's the time when life *actually* happens, when we connect with our surroundings, our loved ones, and ourselves in deep and meaningful ways. But all-too often, the true magic of it gets overlooked, buried under the weight of the past and the angst or dread of the future.

This phase of your self-led journey is designed to develop your inner pause button, so you can more fully engage with the priceless gift of the present. Its exercises will help shift your focus back to the present moment when you're in situations that tempt you to time travel. You will look practically at those challenges, devise plans, and arm yourself with some very practical tools to settle back into here and now. You will also discover the incredible tools you *already* have at your disposal that you can channel to live your life more fully. It's time for you to build a solid foundation for a more fulfilled life grounded in awareness, acceptance, and presence of mind, body, and spirit.

As you have learned so far in this book, our memories and the perceptions we developed from living out our experiences tend to make our worries feel bigger and our fears feel stronger. These have the power to block our ability to truly embrace the present moment. We get stuck obsessing about what went wrong in the past or what will be in the future. Obviously, we want to make improvements on our past and have goals for the future. But when that's our primary focus, we miss out on a lot of that magic I described. When we *only* focus on our goals or correcting past mistakes, we have a hard time living our best life in the present. Spotting these tendencies is an important step toward breaking free from time traveling. Linda shares her story of how this works.

> *As I walked into the bride's room to start getting ready for my wedding, that was the moment I realized I needed to make significant changes in my life. Rather than focusing on how amazing my soon-to-be husband Ryan is, the beautiful pocket scrapbook of our best times that he surprised me with, the intoxicating smell of my bridal flowers, and the love of my family and best friends surrounding me, I got hit with a wave of angst. Maybe the anxiety is more accurately described as a tsunami of emotions.*
>
> *Why do I always get like that? Whenever things are good and calm and happy, something inside me, sort of like a switch, goes off—telling me that I shouldn't get too excited. It says, Nothing good ever lasts. A nudging feeling of waiting for the ball to drop, for the fantasy to end.*
>
> *I started looking for things to pick at, like how the colors of the bridesmaids' dresses didn't exactly match the flowers. I started a fight with my sister about stupid things. I ruminated about the argument with Ryan a few months earlier, wondering if it's a sign we are not compatible. Would the future be full of stupid fights like that? Why do I always do this?*
>
> *There is something wrong with me! I wish I had been able to focus on all the good that was happening around me. But even when I tried a gratitude exercise, there was a voice inside me that felt increasing shame instead of relief. My nitpicking on everything continued on our honeymoon and when we got back to our apartment. It's been just over a month since our wedding and I'm so worried that, if I can't break free of this tendency, I will ruin my marriage before it has a chance to even start!*

I felt so deeply for Linda as she shared her experience. It resonated with me, as a fellow human. The tendency she described is typical for many people, before they learn to process unconscious memories. Once we are aware that we're doing this sort of toxic time travel, we can learn mindfulness techniques and practical strategies to circumvent it. Or we can engage in target memory processing so these triggers don't come up, at all.

Before jumping into present-moment work with Linda, we did a few rounds of EMDR to help her heal the part of her that never felt good enough and the protectors she called "the perfectionist," "the debbie downer," and the "doom and gloom fortuneteller." Similarly, after you do some healing from your past, you will have more resources to face the present.

Linda had somatic symptoms like muscle tension and jaw clench-ing that lessened significantly once she stopped beating herself up about not being fully present at her wedding. She recognized the roots of this tendency—but more importantly, she embraced the idea that she has a long life journey to navigate. The ups and downs and imper-fections are human, par for the course. Seeing this, she was ready to make each moment count.

It's not just the big moments like weddings and holidays we tend to get trapped in and triggered by. We all have day-to-day challenges with the potential to trip us up and throw us off kilter. Let's dig into some of the typical scenarios most of us deal with in our everyday lives.

Common Daily Challenges That Cause Anxiety and Stress

Each day, we face a mixed bag of challenges: some we can see, some are hidden; some come from the outside world, others come from within. The challenges can be physical, like tackling health troubles or navi-gating a tough job. They could also be emotional, like managing a mounting stress load or dealing with a tricky relationship. The unique combination of challenges we face helps us become who we are and ultimately sets the stage for our unfolding life story. However, if we don't keep an eye on the way we react to our day-to-day challenges, the heaviness can build up inside us like a collection of weighted bricks in our backpack. Eventually we might get stuck carrying that extra weight unconsciously, which can manifest as harder-to-fix challenges.

Here's a list of three common challenges and the effects they can have. You will likely find that a variety of challenges you experience are not listed or that some of the challenges have completely different implications for you. I urge you to start a new list from scratch in your binder that feels more accurate for you and your current day-to-day challenges.

Common Challenge: Chronic stress

Potential Roots: High-pressure job, financial instability, difficult relationship

Long-Term Implications: Can lead to various health issues, emotional health problems, reduced life satisfaction, complete burnout, social isolation

Current Impact on Well-Being: Migraines, back pain, irritable bowel, either burnt out and withdrawn or hyperfocused and ignoring everyone

Common Challenge: Poor physical health

Potential Roots: Lack of exercise, poor diet, genetic factors, disease

Long-Term Implications: Physical discomfort, lowered immunity, increased susceptibility to diseases, increased weakness, potential immobility

Current Impact on Well-Being: Impacts ability to carry out daily tasks, reduced energy levels, anxiety about chronic illnesses, unable to exercise, socialize, or work when sick; when well we tend to overdo it, which throws us back to square one

Common Challenge: Emotional dysregulation (difficulty managing emotions)

Potential Roots: Lack of emotional education or role modeling, past traumas, increased unprocessed stress

Long-Term Implications: Social isolation, inability to hold onto a job, not being able to accomplish long-term goals

Current Impact on Well-Being: Lots of interpersonal conflicts, impulsive decisions that create bigger problems, overcorrecting by suppressing feelings leads to explosions at innocent people (which leads to more social isolation)

Once we spot the obstacles we tend to stumble upon in our day-to-day lives, we can start to work with them. Read through these challenges again and start to think about the parts of your own inner family. How do they resonate with or react to each challenge? Try to focus on the challenges at face value. Right now, you are not trying to look for the roots of why these challenges come up. You are not even trying to solve anything. Your goal is to practice looking at your general challenges for what they are—without looking backward and without any added emotional charge.

I know, it's the total opposite of what I've been asking you to do so far. But part of EMDR is combining different types of techniques for a more well-rounded outcome. Now that you have learned to diffuse intense emotions and somatic experiences, you can more easily work on cognitive skills, like modifying thoughts and behaviors. It's a skill to notice the experiences you're having without immediately reacting to them. Consider these questions:

- What part of you is triggered by chronic stress? *Maybe it's the part of you that feels you need to do everything perfectly.*

- What part of you is triggered by difficult relationships? *For example, it might be the part of you that feels too quirky or weird to be accepted.*

- What part of you feels it cannot manage big emotions? *Perhaps there's a peace-loving part of you that feels lost amidst too much chaos or stimulation.*

Let's look at how all this comes together, to form a game plan for your EMDR sessions. Creating a game plan for the present might mean mindfully dipping into the past again temporarily. It may be as simple as looking back at your TIPCES logs and noticing connections between the past and the present challenges. When we can figure out where our most pressing problems tend to stem from, we can then craft ways to bravely face them in the moment.

Your Game Plan for Addressing Your Challenges

Let's say you are a workaholic and no matter what job you've had, you end up going above and beyond to prove yourself. Only you burn out quickly, get sick often, and grow to resent coworkers. It's an ingrained pattern you somehow picked up from your mom because she also moves like the Energizer Bunny…and then crashes. We'll call this part the "Workaholic."

You grew up with the attitude that stress is a status symbol. If you aren't stressed, you aren't doing enough. In reality, you would be far more productive if you got organized, delegated, set boundaries with your time, and set more doable work goals. So why is there a part inside that feels shame if you actually succeed at pacing yourself? This protector part of you does not respect people who take it easy even if you, as your core self, do. Let's call this protector part the "Drill Sargent."

This challenge is that the Drill Sargent part unconsciously makes a connection between being calm with laziness or never-enoughness. You may set goals—like phone curfews, refusing extra work not in your job description, or not taking work home with you—in order to break patterns of workaholism. But this Drill Sargent might punish you and judge you for your new behaviors. Those new goals would only realistically be followed to fruition when once you go back and deal with those parts that judge your new lifestyle goals.

You can create a game plan for how you will work with this. It might look like this:

Common Challenge: Chronic stress

Parts Involved: The Workaholic and The Drill Sargent

Misguided Beliefs: If I'm not stressed, I'm not doing enough, I'm lazy, and I won't amount to anything

New Beliefs: I can accomplish a lot at a healthy, sustainable pace because I am worthy of receiving nourishing rest and calm

Potential Game Plan: Schedule resting time; practice setting boundaries on when and how I work; learn to ask for help with tasks

Essentially, you are connecting to the history of why a pattern keeps coming up, processing it, and making a practical game plan to make real changes in the present. These changes might involve boosting communication skills, deciding on some personal limits, or maybe even getting some relationship counseling. Here are more common challenges to consider. I've connected them with potential parts involved and presented a possible game plan for handling each of them once your processing is done.

Common Challenge: Chronic stress

Parts Involved: The Perfectionist

Misguided Beliefs: I will not be loved and appreciated unless I do x, y, and z

New Beliefs: I am loveable the way I am. I can only do my best.

Potential Game Plan: Create boundaries, deciding what's most important in my life and prioritizing those meaningful things

Common Challenge: Difficult relationships

Parts Involved: The Pariah

Misguided Beliefs: I scare people away and will never keep a solid relationship going because I am too much for other people to handle

New Beliefs: I am worthy of love and will find someone who appreciates my quirks; I can improve my relationship skills

Potential Game Plan: Improve communication skills, set boundaries, consider relationship counseling, and nurture positive relationships in my life

The game plan you come up with can be more detailed than these, with practical and actionable steps you plan to take to improve your situation. For example, to actually create boundaries, you need to write them down in your binder in specific terms like these.

- Don't answer the phone from 8 p.m. to 8 a.m., unless it's my spouse or the kids

- Tell my boss that I won't be able to answer work calls on weekends, but I will check email once a day and respond within 24 hours

- It's too hard to hear what the kids are trying to say to me when they are shouting. I'll explain to them that I'm happy to listen when they are speaking in a quiet and respectful tone.

When you make plans for self-care, take the time to schedule it in your daily planner. Consider listing specific activities that help you recharge and how often you need to do them to maintain emotional well-being. Look for ways to preemptively minimize chaos in your life so you can create moments of meaning and connection. Making a game plan that works calls on your patience, adaptability, and getting to know yourself well. You can always change and adjust the plan as you go along, revising them as your needs change. The goal here is to be very practical about making some real, actionable changes so you can live each day with less anxiety and stress, being more fully in the present moment.

A key part of your overall game plan involves spotting and using your internal and external resources. Learning to take advantage of them will benefit the ongoing development of your healthy lifestyle. In therapeutic terms, we call this *resourcing*. Resourcing allows you to gather up all your strengths, both inside and out, in order to achieve lasting shifts. Your resources are your lifelines, your personal superpowers. They can be innate or acquired qualities.

Internal Resources: Harness Your Strengths

You already possess powerful internal resources. You may recognize them in the following list. After reading through these resources, in your binder list the ones that resonate with you and rate them from 1 to 5, choosing 5 to indicate a superpower, 1 to identify something you're still developing, or any number in between.

Resilience: Bouncing back after tough times

Optimism: Maintaining hope in adversity

Organization: Staying on top of tasks

Determination: Sticking to goals

Self-Worth: A strong sense of value

Personability: Appreciating the good in others

Loyalty: Strong commitment to those you care about

As you identify your internal resources, focus on strengths you already have, not the ones you wish you had. These are your best tools because they are inherently yours. Once you have written down your inner resources, pick three to five resources you value most. In your planner or journal, break them down by strategizing how to harness their potential. For example:

Resilience: I bounce back from adversity quickly

Ideas to Harness This Resource: Practice self-care, use positive self-talk, and step outside my comfort zone occasionally to build even more resilience

Optimism: I maintain hope even in tough times

Ideas to Harness This Resource: Focus on the positive aspects, keep a gratitude journal, stay balanced, and avoid toxic positivity

Determination: I have a strong will to achieve my goals

Ideas to Harness This Resource: Set SMART goals that are specific, measurable, achievable, relevant, and time-bound; celebrate small wins; focus my energy on the right goals

Self-Worth: I know my value isn't defined by others

Ideas to Harness This Resource: Reinforce my self-worth through self-compassion and focusing on fulfillment, not just achievements

Emotional Sensitivity: I can tune into my own and others' emotions

Ideas to Harness This Resource: Set boundaries with others' emotions and nurture my emotional intelligence

Even traits that can be seen as weaknesses, like emotional sensitivity or ADHD, can be strengths if harnessed properly. For example, an "ADHD personality" can be a huge asset when channeled in the right ways.

External Resources: Gain Support from the Outside

External resources are people, places, and things that help you grow. These can be supportive friends, mentors, professional services, or even a calming environment like a favorite beach or garden. Recognizing these resources and leveraging them helps manage challenges and foster growth. Here are some examples.

Supportive Network: Friends, family, neighbors, and colleagues who uplift you

Ideas to Harness These Resources: Strengthen relationships by identifying actions that offer mutual support and appreciation

Mentors: People who offer wisdom and guidance

Ideas to Harness These Resources: Regularly check in with them, be accountable to them for achieving your goals, and show appreciation for their support

Professional Services: Therapy and coaching

Ideas to Harness These Resources: Proactively use sessions to address key issues and then implement feedback and tools

Social Communities: Book groups, podcasts, social media, and online groups

Ideas to Harness These Resources: Schedule time daily to integrate insights into your life, save helpful resources, and discuss them with others

Nature: The beach, a public garden, your backyard, hiking trails

Ideas to Harness These Resources: Schedule a regular time each week to visit nature in order to connect and recharge

Journals: Write down thoughts, sketch meaningful things, or paint in vivid colors

Ideas to Harness These Resources: For clarity and emotional support, set a consistent routine and explore creative journaling styles

Once you identify both internal and external resources, the next step is prioritizing them. It can feel overwhelming, so focus on what is important to you as part of your core values. Then you'll be able to manage your energy and time effectively.

Aligning Daily Life with Your Values

When life feels packed with too many tasks, it had be hard to focus on what matters most. Your core values offer you a personal compass, guiding your thoughts, actions, and decisions. They remind you of what's truly important—what brings purpose and meaning to your life. By staying connected to your values, you can prioritize what truly matters and avoid getting caught in a whirlwind of endless to-dos. Values help you make better choices and stay balanced, especially when you're feeling overwhelmed. They keep you from getting pulled into what others think is important and help you focus on what aligns with your heart. This reduces stress and helps your nervous system stay grounded.

Core values can be anything: honesty, empathy, self-reliance, knowledge, creativity, exploration. To identify or reconnect with your values, spend a few quiet moments reflecting on what matters most to you. This list will likely evolve over time, and that's okay. Here is a helpful, yet quick and easy personal core values assessment you can do right now.

1. Write down up to five values you can think of, off the top of your head, that you believe are most important to you.

2. With a pencil, circle what you believe to be the *top two* values on your list. Then write them in order of importance.

3. Wait a day or two before revisiting your list. Ask yourself if these values feel true and consistent with the kind of person you are and the kind of person you want to be. If they are, you will use them to make decisions. If not, consider the other values you wrote down. With your pencil, put a star by them and keep coming back to the list until you feel you have truly identified your core values.

4. Practice acting in alignment with your values by writing down three actions that they inspire or inform. This will help you make wiser choices, in the present moment and for your future self.

Identifying your values leads to real growth. When you align your daily tasks with what you care about, your life feels more purposeful and your nervous system stays calmer. Tasks aligned with your values are less likely to stress you out because they become an expression of who you are, rather than a burden.

Of course, this isn't always easy. Some essential tasks may not align with your values. Or you might find that even though something is important, you just can't manage it right now. When you take on too much in life, some of it can unintentionally clash with your values and create stress. That's why your values are your best decision-making tool for staying focused on what's truly important without overloading yourself. You can't do it all, and that's okay. Living in alignment with your values is an ongoing process of discovery, adjustment, and reflection. It creates harmony between your inner world and the world around you, making you more productive, grounded, and at peace. It's a challenging but rewarding journey.

Congratulations on all the work you've done to identify your values and begin living more intentionally. With the present-moment tools you have learned in this chapter, you're grounded, steadied, and ready to shift your focus toward the future. Facing it doesn't need to be filled with worry, anxiety, and stress. With a few tools, it can become inspiring and motivating. So let's look ahead. The future awaits!

Mapping the Future

It's completely natural to feel anxious about what lies ahead, especially when you think about the challenges that have caused you stress in the past. But remember, challenges don't have to break you—they can actually be chances to grow stronger. The key isn't to try to banish your worries altogether. That's impossible. Instead, you can learn to handle them with grace, resilience, and deep trust in yourself.

Imagine you're a painter standing before a fresh, white canvas, ready to make your first stroke. It's exciting, isn't it? That's you, standing on the edge of the future—a world full of endless possibilities and new adventures. Each decision, every action, and all the experiences you have add to the masterpiece of your life. Even the mistakes—those *oops* moments—can become some of the most beautiful parts of you, revealing their true meaning as your story unfolds.

This final phase turns your attention toward the future. With all the wisdom you've gained, the self-awareness you've built, and the tools you've gathered, you're now ready to shape a future that reflects your strength and resilience, and embraces life's challenges as opportunities for growth. Up until now, I've encouraged you to stay present, focused on what's here and now, because worrying about the future pulls you away from living fully in the moment. But here's the twist: you *can* look ahead, but instead of focusing on fear or dread, imagine approaching the future like a blank canvas—full of potential.

Shifting from Anxiety to Promise

The Fortune Teller part of you can sometimes predict risks or dangers, and it's okay to use that part to help you prepare. But don't let it run the show. You can connect with this protector part and learn to work with it. Instead of letting it overwhelm you, The Fortune Teller can help you plan for the future without getting stuck in worry. The key is to create a sense of calm in the face of what's to come.

It's important to recognize when you're operating from The Fortune Teller part, rather than your true, core self. As we discussed in chapter 6, the core self is calm, hopeful, patient, and present. If you're feeling tense, anxious, or overwhelmed, it's likely that a protective part has taken over. That's okay—it's human. But as Lila's story shows, you can notice when this happens and gently bring yourself back into contact with your core self. Then you can make decisions with clarity and compassion.

Lila applied the tools you have learned and experienced an incredible transformation in how she managed her anxiety. Six months later, she shared how she continues to grow and navigate life with more ease. Her story is a beautiful example of what happens when we give ourselves permission to trust the process and move forward with hope.

My anxiety has been in such a good place lately. I've been more present with my family, leaving work by 5:30 p.m. most days and enjoying social gatherings without the old worries. I even cleaned out drawers I'd been avoiding for years. Without anxiety dominating my life, I feel more satisfied and engaged in everything, and my physical symptoms—migraines, back pain, arthritis—are gone. My relationship with my siblings has improved too.

But this week, old symptoms resurfaced. I got migraines, my back went out, and I started having stomach issues. I couldn't figure out what was happening, so I reviewed my TIPCES logs and noticed a pattern: each health flare-up involved my sister judging me. I've felt closer to her recently, but I couldn't shake the feeling that something was off.

After some reflection and a few sessions of EMDR Butterfly Hug tapping, I remembered a conversation during a family vacation when my sister commented on my daughter's size and suggested ways to keep thin. I've been working hard to help my children develop healthy body image and avoid dieting pressures, so this hit me hard. I was worried my sister's views on health could influence my daughter, especially as her body changes.

We had an upcoming holiday family gathering that my sister and nieces would also attend. I realized it was bringing up concerns about their eating habits and how they might affect my daughter. But as I tapped and processed, I realized my real issue wasn't just the concern for my daughter—it was feeling judged by my sister, and even by myself. Once I identified the root of the anxiety, I felt huge relief.

With that clarity, I was able to plan for the gathering in a calm, practical way—focusing on what I could control. The event turned out to be wonderful, and I'm so grateful for having tools to navigate my anxiety. I feel like I've regained control over my life.

This is exactly the outcome to hope for when embracing and channeling our inner fortune teller. As Lila's story shows, with a little TIPCES detective work, anxiety triggers are pretty easily grouped and rearranged into new clusters. Our anxious and fearful parts often hang out together in groups, around common themes or patterns that we can easily spot in order to find the problems and then develop solutions. I'm so excited for you to begin this next phase, where you can start shaping your future with the same strength, compassion, and wisdom that you've cultivated so far. You've got this.

Prepare for Inevitable Challenges

Now it's your turn. What patterns motivate the anxieties you tend to feel? To find these groupings, write down your current anxieties while considering related past memories. Can you spot any patterns or recurring themes? Understanding these patterns helps us predict possible anxiety triggers in future scenarios, helping us get ready to tackle our jitters *before* they show up.

Some events and situations are like anxiety magnets, universally famous for waking up our anxious parts. Consider how family get-togethers, holidays, and big life changes like marriage, relationship breakups, moving, or changing jobs affect your anxiety. Because these predictable anxiety magnets are the easiest to identify, they are simpler to be proactive about. You don't need to play guessing games. Lila knew her sister was coming to visit. It wasn't a surprise. She just had to dig into her reactions to locate the specifics so she could do the work beforehand, coming up with plans to help her get through their time together. When the visit took place, she was prepared with tools to keep her mind level and her body grounded. Wouldn't having that foresight be helpful? You can get there too.

Follow the Patterns to See What's Coming

Knowing about these triggers in advance is ideal, but not always possible. That's okay. Even when we don't know exactly what will happen, if we follow the patterns, we can make pretty accurate predictions. For example, if you know that you are afraid of bees you can bet that at some point in your life you will be face to face with a buzzing yellow fluff ball and her stinger. You can't prevent it if you are a healthy person who goes outside their house. So what can you do to prepare for the ultimate face-off? It depends on your preferences.

- There are exercises you could try to put your fear in perspective, drawn from cognitive behavioral therapy (CBT)

- To move and release the energy of your anxiety and stress, the tapping method of emotional freedom technique (EFT) might help

- If you aren't traumatically scared of bees, you could visit a bee farm to become more informed and apply insights from exposure therapy in a controlled environment

- Read blogs about strategies or watch YouTube videos by people who have faced the same issue

- Meet with a therapist to talk through thoughts that are intrusive and debilitating

My point is, certain experiences are inevitably going to become an issue. If your anxiety about facing these things in the future gives you stomach pains and keeps you up at night, you can take control and make a plan. The following sections offer helpful ways to get ready for predictable stressors. You got this!

Think Like an Event Planner

Event planners are pros at preemptively solving problems. With years of practice, they learn to plan for almost anything that may come up. They know what first-aid items need to be stocked in their handbags; they have lists of backups if a regular vendor doesn't show up; they have pep talks prepared for the hosts in case they get anxious. Event planners rock at predicting the unpredictable.

You can learn to think like an event planner. Think ahead to a common scenario or a big event coming up in your life. Consider these questions:

- In what ways could you predict things going wrong?

- What will cause your inner alarms to flare?

- How might your anxious parts show up in this situation?

Draw on What Went Well

Another way to identify how you can prepare for an upcoming, anxiety-triggering event or situation is to follow your own bread trail. Think about other times in your life when you were put in a similar situation—and it went well. What did you do differently that time?

- Maybe you had a buddy who was in charge of not leaving your side, who could change potentially triggering conversation topics

- Perhaps you found that a short visit is less likely to become triggering, so you limited your exposure to a half hour

- A helpful mantra could have repeated in your mind to keep you focused, and perhaps you can come up with more things to say to yourself during the event

In your binder or journal, record your observations. It's likely that your own experience navigating life offers great ideas for what may work for you ongoing. Then you can intentionally prepare for challenges, using these tools.

Experiment with New Possibilities

If you have never experienced success when facing this particular challenge, you can come up with some experiments to try. Look at the whole event as a scientific study and try to identify variables. Make hypotheses. It can be a fun experiment, if you let it! Here are the steps to take.

1. In your journal or binder, write down an upcoming event or scenario that has the potential to go wrong and cause your anxious parts to go haywire

2. Make a list of ten strategies you could try, drawing on the resources and tools you have gathered so far

3. Try each one out and see what happens, recording which ones work and which ones don't

4. Write down any new strategies you may come up with, adding more ideas to this list as you live and learn

As you continue to experiment and sharpen your practice of applying these strategies, this personalized anxiety first-aid toolbox can become one of your most prized possessions. By understanding what might trigger your anxiety and how it affects you, then learning to anticipate these possible glitches, you can save yourself from lots of suffering and pain in life. Cultivating an inner event planner can help you prepare for better outcomes as you get ready to face these situations with more courage and calm.

A Foundation of Strength and Confidence

In this phase, we've taken a good look at gearing up for future speed bumps. We unpacked the idea of predicting future triggers by identifying common denominators among our memory clusters and practiced ways to build up individualized toolboxes of strategies to prepare for life's blips. As Lila's story showed, we can always apply EMDR-style methods when we need them. More awareness of the past can help with future predictions and fill the toolbox with strategies to use whenever we need them.

By using the power of planning ahead to prep, you can lay a strong foundation for your mental health that enables you to face the future with increased strength and confidence. You're now armed and ready with the knowledge and tools to not just survive life's speed bumps, but to thrive in the midst of them. You can carve out a future that reflects your strengths, values, and dreams.

This journey toward self-improvement and better mental health is more like a marathon than a sprint. When we stick with it and stay committed, it may be tough, but the reward is a life of improved mental well-being and personal fulfillment. That's definitely worth the effort.

Checking In and Tuning Up

We would never expect a car to run smoothly without regular check-ups and tune-ups. A garden won't bloom without pruning and consistent watering. So why do we expect our minds and bodies to stay strong and vibrant without regular effort? Reevaluating the progress we have made and making plans for maintenance are as important as any other phase so far. The steps of reevaluation and rejuvenation set this self-guided EMDR method apart from one-off solutions to specific problems. Many methods are great to get over a hump…but then what? All too often, the progress we make in self-help ends up withering over time because we stop sticking to our plans. This phase can offer you the ultimate "choose your own adventure" journey through life. With this book, you can create lifelong connections with your inner world that you will continue *wanting* to nurture and strengthen as time goes on. Then you will keep the flame going.

Nurturing and Raising Your Parts

Like children craving connection, our anxious parts benefit greatly from regular check-ins. This is a normal human need and not necessarily a maladaptive, needy one. If you are a parent, every day you likely ask your child how school went or whether they were able to resolve a conflict with their friend. That's just a normal thing to do. Think of your journey through this book as you repaired any attachment deficits I described in chapter 3 by fostering a nurturing parental connection with your inner parts. To explore this more, let's look further at parent-child dynamics.

If you have human children with strong personalities, you know how fragile the relationship with them can get when you are not in your game—neglecting self-care to the point that your nerves are fried. A screaming, stubborn child has the potential to totally derail your equilibrium. You can't afford to scream and yell back if you want your child to be emotionally healthy and strong. You would never try to shut your child up in an abrasive way. Nor would you want to convey the message that they have to be small or hide or suppress their needs and desires if they want you to love them. Your job as a parent is to help that intensity, strong-will, and passion be expressed, grow, and flourish in a way that will benefit the child. Parents need to model emotional regulation consistently. The same is true for parenting your inner parts.

Just like human children, your anxious child parts have fundamental needs that must be seen and heard. Yes, they keep you on your toes, helping you stay alert to potential dangers. But they also have very real sensitivities and often deeply rooted pain. So it's no wonder that no matter how pesky you might find these parts, their voices don't go away when you ignore them. If you never learned to truly listen to what they are trying to say, like a real child, they will just keep getting louder and louder and more desperate. The longer you disregard what they are trying to tell you, the worse your symptoms of anxiety and stress will be.

Now that you have worked through the previous phases and hopefully forged a stronger bond with your anxious parts, I hope you are beginning to crave ongoing connection with them. Awareness of your child parts strengthens the bond that can keep your inner and outer world in sync. Ultimately, you want to remain firmly in your rightful role, as the core self—the parent, guide, and mentor for your inner world. By becoming more emotionally regulated in this core self, your anxious parts will come around and begin to enjoy being loved, taken care of, and mentally snuggled as helpful members of your inner family. Like a kind parent, try speaking gently to your parts, hear their objections and complaints, offer them perspective on their struggles, and guide them to make wise choices. Every day offers new opportunities for your inner world to work together in meaningful ways.

With this book's hands-on approach to well-being, your thoughts, feelings, and actions can match up with your core values. You have worked so hard to get to this point and I hope you know how good life can be now. You can achieve so much when you are focused on the present moment and only use time travel for information that serves your growth. With this newfound awareness and the support of your many inner parts, you have the power to tackle problems while they're still small. Successfully doing this involves maintenance work.

Schedule Check-Ups with Yourself

Maintenance work might not seem as exciting as the discovery phase of your journey. But like any relationship, once the honeymoon stage has passed, fulfillment comes down to the day-to-day grind, the small choices you make every day that add up over time and help you live your best life. Your relationship with your inner world is no different. The ability to look back at your regular gratitude journal entries when you aren't feeling all that grateful will keep you going. Drawing on your newfound awareness will keep you grounded when things are joyous and will offer the tools to get back to equilibrium when you get thrown off kilter. But honestly, the small steps and the tiniest one-off choices— like choosing to meditate for a few minutes each day, selecting a healthier meal for dinner even if it's "just this once," taking a short walk, using Butterfly Hug tapping to get through a problem—make the biggest difference to our mental health in the long run.

To support this maintenance work, draw on EMDR's reevaluation stage to deliberately check in with yourself, almost as if discussing the effects of your inner work with a therapist. How are your *distress levels* throughout the day? Are *strong positive cognitions* present in how you speak about your experience and how you talk to yourself? Would processing a new target memory be helpful? What goals would you like to work on next? To do this, you will need to schedule specific dates when you will check in with yourself and reevaluate your progress. The frequency is totally up to you, perhaps once a week or once a month. Whatever your schedule will allow is great, as long as it is doable for you. Consistency is key. The last thing you want to do is make a plan that you know you can't implement.

Take a moment to reflect and decide how much time you realistically can devote to maintenance work for your mental health. Each session will probably take around an hour, depending on how much you plan to cover. Book it now! Schedule that time in your planner. You won't regret it. This time will become sacred for you. Here's an idea for how to make the most of your check-in.

Exercise: Your Reevaluation Session

You are going to play the role of both therapist and client in this exercise, so get your imagination wheels turning. Envision that you are a therapist sitting across from your client (also you) in cozy chairs. This therapist looks like you, and is you, so you already have a close connection. For effect, I suggest that you move from chair to chair as you play both parts. When you are speaking as the therapist, sit in one chair. When you are speaking as the client, sit on another chair or switch positions on a big comfy couch. This exercise is much more effective if you are talking out loud. It may feel silly at first but try visualizing it as a performance. Whatever helps make the exchange more comfortable.

Begin by imagining you are in a warm and cozy room. It's your ideal setting for relaxation, decorated in the style you like the most. Maybe there is a fireplace and a chunky knitted blanket you can wrap yourself up in. Perhaps there's a mountain view and portraits of horses on the wall. Or maybe the room is a fresh, bright color with lots of beautiful plants and boho wall hangings. Close your eyes for a minute or two to really visualize it. You are visiting your dream therapist's office, so make it good!

As therapist-you, begin asking questions. The goal is to reevaluate and check in with client-you, making sure that all your hard work is still effective. Curious to find out if there are any symptoms, behaviors, or reactions to triggers that can be explored further, therapist-you wants to hear any new thoughts, epiphanies, insights, or information. Then offer support for new goal setting or current challenges that have been causing problems. Here are some questions that can be posed by therapist-you.

- Since our last check-in, what have you noticed in your day-to-day life? Any changes, positive or negative?

- How has the last target memory we processed been feeling inside you?

- What comes up for you now when you start to think about it?

- When you think about it, what are you visualizing?

- What emotions are coming up? What sensations are you feeling?

- Have you had any insights or epiphanies about that memory recently?

If you really want to be authentic, therapist-you can even pull out a clipboard and jot down important notes. Let client-you take all the time needed to think through and answer the questions fully. Like a real therapy session, you don't want to rush things.

Whenever client-you brings up distressing thoughts, emotions, or feelings, do a quick SUDS scale assessment and body scan. Here are some prompts to help.

- On a scale of 0 to 10, where 0 is no disturbance at all or just neutral and 10 is the most disturbance you can possibly imagine, how disturbing does this thought feel to you now?

- Where do you feel that disturbance in your body? What is it doing? Where is it going? Describe it.

Therapist-you will then check in on client-you's validity of cognition (VOC). Remember how in phase 2 you shifted unhelpful core beliefs toward new helpful cognitions? With the VOC check-in, you can ensure that the newer, more helpful beliefs still feel very true (significantly truer than your initial negative ones). You want to make sure that your new healthy belief systems are firmly rooted. Therapist-you can do this by asking the following question.

- When you think of the memory now, reframed with your new helpful cognition, how true do the words feel to you now? Rate them on a scale from 1 to 7, where 1 feels completely false and 7 feels completely true.

If the processing of the target memory appears well and good, that's amazing! You can then turn toward creating some SMART goals that are specific, measurable, achievable, relevant, and time-bound. Or decide on your next target memory, evaluate a recent trigger, or explore a symptom that you want to process next. If there is still disturbance, you have some tweaking to do. If an old unhelpful core belief is rearing its ugly head, you need to do a bit more detective work. Therapist-you can explore whether the challenge keeping you stuck lies in the past, present, or future by asking questions like these.

- Are you triggered by something that feels familiar to you, but you can't quite figure out what it is (past)?

- Are you having specific challenges coping during the day (present)?

- Are you worried about something coming up (future)?

If therapist-you has a hard time getting to the bottom of it, client-you can try the butterfly hug first and then let the mind wander a bit. Coupled with a quick body scan, the following questions might do the trick!

- Close your eyes and focus on the incident you are thinking about and what's going on inside you. Mentally scan your entire body and notice where the disturbances are located. What qualities do they have?

- Notice the thoughts, feelings, and emotions going on. Is there any familiarity? Does any sensation remind you of another memory?

- Breathe into the disturbance through your nose, giving it some much-needed oxygen. And then breathe out whatever stress and worry it's carrying through your mouth. Do any insights arise?

You can also look through your TIPCES logs and see if you can find some common factors in your log entries that recur. These can offer clues to whatever might be going on for you. Lila's story in phase 4 was a great example of how to do this. Once client-you has made a discovery, therapist-you can consider which of the exercises from the past, present, and future phases might help. Then create a new game plan and set it in motion.

If client-you is still feeling disturbance at this point, it's okay, especially if you did some great work. When inner shifts happen, it's normal to feel a bit disoriented. It can take time and effort for new responses to triggers to come readily to you in the moment or take effect. End your reevaluation session with the containment exercise from chapter 1 or some grounding techniques from chapter 8. Now pat yourself on the back. I'm sure that wasn't easy.

A Lifelong Process of Flexibility in the Face of Change

Personal growth isn't a race, and perfection isn't necessary—just consistent effort. Life will always throw you surprises, and you can embrace being flexible while staying committed to meaningful actions. Personally, I feel really accomplished right now, something the old me never would have acknowledged. Back then, before I began engaging the tools offered in this book, I'd get overwhelmed by long to-do lists and stop before even trying. But now, I'm proud of the progress I've made and excited for what's ahead.

In life, we must adapt and adjust, and learning to do that gracefully is a powerful resilience skill. It's normal to start something with enthusiasm, only to lose momentum over time. We mess up, procrastinate, and sometimes quit—but we always get back up. This cycle often happens when the honeymoon phase of a new goal fades, and we're faced with the choice to either let it go—or recommit and adjust our plan.

We never stay stagnant; we move up, down, forward, and backward. Knowing this, it makes sense to plan for setbacks, right? Some people call this "falling off the wagon," but that phrase can feel limiting. It's often used for addictive behaviors, implying that we should always be "on the wagon." But what if "falling off" isn't failure? What if eating a piece of cake is part of your plan—bringing joy and nostalgia instead of shame? Savoring that moment at your child's birthday party can be more valuable than adhering to a rigid rule.

What if you didn't have to constantly rise and fall, succeed or fail? What if every step—whether direct or winding—was just part of the journey? Life would certainly be less stressful.

This is why regular check-ins with yourself, to see how you're doing and revisit your goals, are so important. Don't let shame hold you back. Appreciate where you are in the process. Shaming yourself for not being perfect will only keep you stuck. If sticking to your goals feels hard, it doesn't mean change is impossible. It's a sign to adjust your plan. Growth is a journey, and celebrating small successes along the way will keep you going.

Physical activity also plays a huge role in our ability to manage our inner world. Many of us associate exercise with stress, but when we focus on joyful movement—whether it's dancing or walking—it can be energizing and grounding. Joyful movement has so many benefits, from boosting mood to reducing stress and improving brain function. Even light movement can reverse stress damage and help your body handle stress more effectively. Find ways to move every day that you enjoy. It makes a world of difference.

I'm excited for you. You've already made incredible progress, and with the tools you've gained, you can keep moving forward. Just like tweaking a car when it's not running perfectly, we can make small adjustments in our growth process. Breathing exercises, grounding practices, or quick self-therapy sessions can all help reduce stress in the moment. Maintaining boundaries can help you devote energy to what's important to you. Not every tool works for every situation, so it's important to experiment and find what works best for you. The same goes for mantras, mindfulness, and other techniques—choose the ones that genuinely help and tweak them as needed. The coming chapters offer many quick first-aid tips and power tools to help you stay on track.

Part Four

Tools for Ongoing Resilience

Chapter 8

Grounding and Reorienting Tools

Your mind may start to time travel to the past or the future at inopportune times. Or you could get stuck in a shame spiral, when even though you prioritize activities according to your values, you still feel overwhelmed. It's important to have ways to settle your nervous system and bring you back to the present moment. Having grounding and reorienting techniques in your toolbox are essential for being healthy and strong in the present.

Sometimes we can get disoriented when we do deep therapeutic work, whether on our own or with a therapist. It's normal to feel wobbly after clearing out old, deeply rooted distortions. Be mindful of this when trying techniques on your own. You won't have a therapist there to remind you to reestablish a connection to the here and now. Each time you finish a round of EMDR, you will want to check in to make sure you are grounded in the present moment.

Grounding techniques use your senses or thoughts to refocus on what's happening right now. They could involve paying attention to your breathing, touching an object to feel its texture, or picturing a calm and beautiful place. These techniques are like anchors that keep you steady when the world feels a bit wobbly.

Reorienting techniques, on the other hand, help you recognize your place in space, time, and in relation to other people. Acknowledging how you're connected to your surroundings, the current moment, and those around you can boost your sense of presence and safety.

You learned about polyvagal theory in chapter 2, when I described how your nervous system responds to stress and the role your vagus nerve plays in regulating it. When you think about it, it makes sense that consciously relaxing your muscles and controlling your breathing rate sends a signal to your parasympathetic nervous system that you've got things under control (Porges 2018). When your breathing is calm and relaxed, your face muscles loosen and you release tension from different parts of your body. This makes your internal alarm bells much less likely to trip or trick you into time traveling. Even when you have annoying thoughts, if you are able to get your body—or just your face muscles—to become calm and purposefully relaxed, you are far less likely to experience anxiety symptoms. Learning to do this is important because if these symptoms become chronic, they can damage your body and will eventually fry your internal alarm system so that it is always on high alert.

As you will see, these tools are not very complicated. Many people find relief after a simple shift in awareness. It's especially effective to practice these techniques regularly when you are feeling good and grounded, so that when you need them in a pinch during stressful situations, you're already a pro. When using your power tools is second nature to you, it's a good sign you have successfully built up strong emotional health and resilience muscles.

Breathwork Grounding Exercises

Breathwork is a valuable tool for both mental and physical health, as it can help improve lung function and be a great way to ground yourself when you feel unsteady. Certain exercises might feel uncomfortable or even triggering for some people, and for others the exact same exercise brings immense relief right away. It's important to observe how each one makes you feel as you try them. Don't force anything if it doesn't feel good. Simply move on to try the next option.

Breathing exercises can be as simple as taking a few moments to yourself and noticing the rhythm of your normal breath. It doesn't take much time out of your day to use breathwork as a strong anchor when you are feeling off, or to help you be more mindful and attuned in any situation. Just set aside time to pay attention to your body and your breathing. Here are a few breathing exercises that I find helpful.

Humming Bee

This type of breathing is meant to create an instantaneous calming sensation while soothing the tension around your forehead. Following these steps can help relieve headaches due to tension, pent up frustration, anxiety, anger, and rage.

1. Find a comfortable seated position. Close your eyes and relax your face, head, neck, and shoulders.

2. Place your pointer fingers on cartilage of both ears, the part that sticks out near your cheek bones. Fold them over to partially protect your ear canal. Inhale for 5 seconds.

3. As you exhale, gently press your fingers into the cartilage to close the gap over the ear canal. With your mouth closed, make a humming sound as you breathe out naturally from the nose. Do this for as long as is comfortable.

4. Keep repeating until the tension settles.

Blow Out the Candles

This type of breathwork can help you develop breathing patterns for activities that require more stamina. It's great to do while you are recovering from a cold or chest congestion, as it can help break up and clear fluids in your lungs. Follow these steps to help slow down your breathing during anxiety attacks or more intense activities like jogging or lifting.

1. Sit up straight, either in a chair, cross-legged, or with legs folded under so you are sitting on your shins. Relax your neck and shoulders while opening up your chest.

2. With your mouth closed, inhale slowly and deeply through your nose and into your belly as you count to 5.

3. Pucker your lips as though you are going to blow out a candle. Exhale hard, yet smoothly, by blowing air from the depths of

your lungs out through your pursed lips. As your lungs empty out, your belly should feel like it's snapping in.

4. Breathe in (don't focus on the inhales, as they will happen naturally), then pucker your lips and blow out. Repeat this three times at a longer length and slower pace.

5. Now try another three rounds with quicker and shorter exhales.

Make sure there's a consistency to the breath pattern. It can be helpful to have someone clap a consistent beat or you can use a metronome app to set the pace. It's normal to cough a bit at first, until you become used to doing this. I recommend practicing so this feels effortless. Then the breath pattern will help when you need it.

Deep Belly Breath

This breathing technique helps you engage and use your diaphragm properly. It's most effective when you're feeling relaxed and rested, so this is more of a proactive power tool than a reactive one. Place a light object on your belly so you can see the way the stomach rises and falls as you breathe deeply.

1. Sit with your legs crossed or in a chair. You can also lie comfortably on your back with your head on a pillow and your knees slightly bent, perhaps supported by a pillow also.

2. With one hand on your upper chest and one hand below your rib cage (over your belly), notice the pace of your breath and how your stomach moves up and down with the support of your diaphragm.

3. Slowly inhale through your nose, feeling your stomach pressing into your hand for 4 to 6 seconds. Keep your other hand still on your chest.

4. Exhale slowly through your mouth, in a loose "O" shape, out from deep, deep down in the lowest part of the lungs where they meet the diaphragm. Imagine the diaphragm is blowing up a strong balloon to push air up and out of your mouth.

5. Simultaneously, the balloon is also pressing downward and you need to tighten your stomach muscles to protect your core. Envision another force, like a corset, wrapping around your lower back and hips, all the way to your front. This tightens your midsection to strengthen your core muscles as added protection from the pressure of the balloon.

When you get better at doing this, you can make this more challenging by choosing a heavier object to place on your stomach. If you have not done this breathing exercise before, you might feel tired at first. Over time it should become easier and feel more natural. Practicing a few times a day, for a few minutes at a time, will make it available when you need it most.

Additional Activities to Try

There are many ways to bring ourselves back into the present moment. It can help to have a range of tools for different situations, emotional reactions, and physical symptoms. Try all of these out to find the ones that work for you in ways you enjoy.

Progressive Muscle Relaxation (PMR): A lot of evidence-based research supports the effectiveness of PMR, and it is also simple to learn. All you have to do is tense and then relax each of the fourteen major muscle groups in your body, one by one (Jacobson 1938). To try PMR, slowly tense and then relax the following parts of your body, in this order: fists, forehead, eyes, jaw, tongue, lips, neck, shoulders, upper back (shoulder blades and back of ribs), biceps (the large muscle on the front inside of the upper arm between the shoulder and the elbow), triceps (the large muscle on the back side of the upper arm, stomach, lower back, buttocks, upper legs, calves, shins, ankles, feet (heel, top bridge, and bottom arch), toes. If you want to, try tensing and relaxing the muscle groups in the reverse order—from your toes up to your head!

Categories: Pick any category of things, like shapes, textures, or colors. Then name all the ones you can currently observe in that category.

The examples I offered are pretty easy. You can make this more engaging by observing a variety of interesting categories. For example, if I'm outside in my yard I might choose the category of nature. In my head, I'd create a list of everything I observe in nature (as opposed to things like buildings and cars). This might include: fresh cut grass, birds chirping, a design in the tree bark, a gooey snail near my foot, annoying flies buzzing around. List as many observations as you can.

Chocolate Kiss: Hold a chocolate kiss in your hand and observe it with different senses. What does the wrapper look like? How does it feel while it's melting in the palm of your hand? What does it smell like? Keep going. Then unwrap the chocolate kiss and put it in your mouth, making more observations with your senses. What is the texture as it slowly melts on your tongue? Does the taste change as you chew? Feel the contraction in your throat as you swallow. This technique is really fun for kids. It can be fun to do the same exercise with an ice cube on a hot day.

Make It Count: Try counting backwards from 20 to 0. Yes, it's as simple as that. You could also do some math equations in your head or practice times tables. I know it could sound funny, but many people find doing this highly reorienting.

Breathe Out the Stress: Take a big breath in, as deep and as long as you can. Imagine that you are inhaling all of the goodies your body needs to be healthy, like fresh oxygen and relaxation. Hold your breath for 8 seconds. As you exhale, imagine that you're breathing out stress and also getting rid of all of the toxins inside you, like carbon dioxide and any germs or infections you may be carrying. Breathe out from deep down inside your lungs, long and slow.

Grounded Connection: Sit in a chair, on the ground, or wherever you feel comfortable. Feel your body connecting to whatever you are sitting on. Bring your attention to how that connection feels as it supports your weight and the specific spots where your body makes contact with the chair, ground, or yoga mat.

Deep Roots: Imagine you are a tree with roots extending from your feet into the ground. Imagine your roots reach deep down into the

Earth, all the way to the middle of the planet. The center of the planet is your anchor. Even when the winds of change and challenge threaten to blow you away, you are deeply and firmly anchored and safe.

Rote Recital: Many people know poems, songs, or psalms by heart. Evidence shows that reciting these verses quietly to yourself or aloud can be very grounding. You can focus on the meaning of each word or how your lips feel as words come out of your mouth. If you decide to recite the words inside your head, visualize each word or even each letter as if you are reading it on paper.

LOL: Surprisingly, this one is difficult for many people. It can be hard to make yourself laugh out loud. Think of, or make up, a funny joke. Recall the details of a funny memory. If you like silly humor, print a page of knock-knock jokes or buy a joke book to keep in your handbag. Watch funny baby and animal reels on social media. If you have time, a comedy movie or television show can make you laugh. In addition to helping to ground you, laughter has so many other healing benefits.

Visualization: When you are feeling dysregulated, imagine the face of your hero or someone you deeply love. Detail all of their positive qualities inside your head. Imagine their face in front of you or their voice speaking to you, telling you what you need to hear. What validating words would they share when you are having a tough moment?

Make Lists: Write in your journal or mentally make a list of as many things you can think of that bring you joy or pleasure. Give yourself a set time to brainstorm, just a few minutes. As you go through the list, meditate on each of the items and think of as much detail as you can.

Movement: Any sort of movement, from light stretches to full-blown cardio exertion, can alleviate anxiety symptoms and ground you. Along with the movement, it's important to pay attention to your breath and any physical sensations that arise. Whether you decide to do jumping jacks, go on a hike, or lie down on the grass to stretch your muscles, notice the grounding effects the activity has on your body. Movement, especially when enjoyable, is a power tool that can reduce anxiety and bring you back to the here and now as you work through a panic attack.

Music: Put on one of your favorite songs. Focus on the lyrics, the melody, or each of the instruments separately. As you listen, notice the body sensations you are having. I personally like to combine music with joyful movement to dance out my stress and anxiety. It can be a really fun and healthy practice!

These techniques are evidence-based gold standards for alleviating both acute and chronic anxiety symptoms. They help settle our nerves during big, intense, overwhelming feelings. When you get stuck with feelings that are intrusive and uncomfortable, grounding techniques offer a powerful way to move through them. The best part is that most of these exercises take only a few minutes to do. You can practice anytime and anywhere, often without other people knowing. These activities have the power to help anchor you in the present while giving your body and mind some balance and respite from what can feel like an endless barrage of anxiety symptoms. You'll feel more present for what matters to you in life. In the next chapter, you'll learn how you can free up even more of your anxious energy so you can choose what you want to focus on.

Chapter 9

Maintain Boundaries for Stress Reduction

Boundaries are essential to any healthy relationship. They have been proven effective in reducing symptoms of stress, depression, and anxiety. Being able to set boundaries is a major component of self-care. With healthy boundaries, we can say "no" to things that are overwhelming for us, which supports our overall health and wellbeing. The boundary problems we tend to face often arise because it can be hard to figure out exactly what we want our boundaries to be. Also, our needs can ebb and flow over time, requiring us to adjust accordingly.

You've learned a lot about the *whys* but not as much about the *hows*. In this chapter, we'll focus your power tools on clarifying your struggles, identifying the boundaries you need to set, as well as applying proactive and reactive methods for boundary setting. You'll find opportunities to practice defining your boundaries and come up with ways to effectively communicate them to others. Use your journal for these exercises.

Before you consider your own experience, I'd like to introduce you to Gary. When Gary came into my office for the first time, it was clear his problems were all about boundaries. Here's how he describes his evolution.

Growing up, I never knew that I had the right to say no or respectfully decline. My parents taught me that in school I had to always listen to my teachers, no matter what. At home, my parents had very unrealistic expectations of me and I felt suffocated. This feeling spilled over into so many of my relationships. I began to hate people in general, if you can imagine. But people all seemed to love me for what I did for them.

At work, I had to be pleasant and accommodating so I held in my resentment and overwhelm until work was over—and then I took it out on my wife. Rita bore the brunt of my anger, hostility, and passive aggressiveness. In hindsight, I feel really bad for her. She stuck with me through all my insanity, bordering on abusive behavior. The worst part was that to the outside world I looked like a saint, the nicest guy in the world. She was always upset at the way I treated her, so people thought she was the miserable and mean one. I still feel awful about it. She threatened to leave me if I didn't get help. I'm so glad she did. Thankfully our relationship has improved since I learned about boundaries and my life is so much better now.

The biggest change was in my relationship with my parents. They were becoming more and more needy, and their expectations of me were completely unrealistic. I grew up with a lot of bible-shaming manipulations about the commandment to honor thy father and mother. Once I learned that it was okay and even necessary to set boundaries with them, my frustration was no longer taken out on Rita. Poor woman.

As I started to set boundaries, parts of me got worried and anxious about setting them. Doing things for people and being a yes-man was part of my persona and I felt that made people like me. A part of me worried that if I started setting boundaries and saying no to people, even though it was best for me and my marriage, I wouldn't be loved. With my parents that anxious feeling was really strong. I needed to explore what parts of me were trying to stand in the way. Even though I managed to set the boundaries with my parents, at first I had very strong physical reactions to doing it.

As Gary's story shows, in order to set boundaries you need to strengthen your boundaries' muscles. By working through the following activities, you'll be off to a good start. Observe your internal dynamics and become curious about why an *anxious part* might try to prevent you from setting certain types of boundaries with certain types of people.

You can also relate to your hesitant or anxious parts by identifying target memories and following the EMDR-style process you learned in phase 2. Here are some important clarifying questions to write about in your journal or binder.

The Need for Boundaries with a Specific Person

Sometimes, we just know when someone is overstepping. Or we have an underlying unease about the dynamic. On a fresh page, write down the name of a person you feel the need to set boundaries with, as part of your relationship. Then answer these questions.

- What is my stress level when this person is around?

- What do they do that causes me anxiety, worry, or stress?

- What might be the trigger or source of my discomfort?

- What might I be missing if I don't set a boundary with them?

- What am I worried will happen if I succeed at setting the boundary?

Areas in Life Where You Need to Set Boundaries

We all have areas of our lives that light us up. For various reasons, we also maintain relationships, tasks, obligations, and even possessions that bring us down emotionally. As you consider the boundaries you need to set, clarify how different areas of your life affect you.

- What people, activities, or things in my life infuse me with energy?

- What people, activities, or things do I encounter that tend to drain me of energy?

- What people, activities, or things makes me feel valued, happy, supported, safe, or…?

- What people, activities, or things make me feel drained, frustrated, defeated, hopeless, or…?

Sketch Out Your Boundaries

Here's a way to visualize what you want in your life, and what you don't. Draw a large circle on a blank sheet of paper. Inside it, write all the things you can think of that make you feel calm, secure, and safe. A few examples include nature walks, hugs from specific people, prayer, a conversation with a good friend over coffee.

Outside the circle, write down all the things that stress you out, make you feel unsafe, or derail your equilibrium. The list will include people or situations that push your boundaries. Examples include: friends gossiping in front of you even after you've asked them not to, your roommate taking your food without permission, a mother-in-law's tendency to drop in unannounced, your boss calling you in non-work hours when you're home, or someone touching you in ways that creep you out.

Practice and Use "I Statements" When Communicating

One of the best snippets of advice for boundary setting is "less is more." When we are unclear with others about our wants and needs, making excuses or offering too many reasons, the message gets lost. When setting boundaries that will hold, simplify what you want to say. No convoluted phrases or sandwiching what you're trying to say with empty or untrue platitudes. When you complicate what you're trying to say, feelings often get hurt. Just pick the main thing that is bothering you, stick to "I statements," and be clear.

Stating what you want is often referred to as an "I statement." Many people can't easily define what they actually *want*. They generally know what they *don't want*—but negative statements rarely create effective boundaries. For others to truly understand what you are asking of them, learn to communicate your wants and needs effectively.

First, review your top values from the work you did in phase 3, and think of ways to protect them from being compromised by setting boundaries. Once you've figured out the areas you would like to set boundaries around, and are preparing to communicate them, don't tiptoe around the subject. Vagueness leaves room for interpretation. Confrontation in an accusatory way creates bad will and causes conflict with backlash you really don't want to deal with later. "I statements" focus on your needs and preferences. It helps you speak your truth to communicate effectively. Practice shifting toward phrases like these.

"I'd like..."

"I'd prefer..."

"I need..."

"I expect..."

Let's explore this with an example. Say you want your mother-in-law to call before she visits. Rather than saying, "Please don't come over without permission," try saying, "I need you to text or call before popping in so we can make sure the time works for both of us." Some common, effective, simple phrases you might want to memorize include:

"I'm not comfortable with this."

"Thank you for reaching out. I can't at this time."

"This doesn't work for me right now."

"I need to draw the line at x, y, and z."

Anatomy of a Good Boundary

When setting boundaries, it doesn't help to shout, whisper, mumble, or make excuses. Knowing what effective and kind boundary setting looks like is helpful. Many of us did not grow up with role models who lived with strong and healthy boundaries. The anatomy of really good boundary setting should have the following qualities.

- Confident, assertive, yet kind body language

- Respectful, firm, clear body language.

- Voice is steady and unapologetic, at an appropriate volume and tone

It's important to point out that compromise, as long as you are not compromising on your values, is not a weakness. Provided you are comfortable with the terms and have worked out a way that the problem won't continue to trigger you, it can work. Give-and-take—or better yet, *give-and-give*—is actually a crucial aspect of healthy relationships.

Whenever you have told someone clearly—more than once—that if a behavior continues, you will have to set even stronger boundaries and they ignore you, they are a repeat offender. It is totally within reason to "ghost" them indefinitely, or until they've proven to you that they are capable of respecting your boundaries. But be discerning about taking such extreme measures. You will want to reserve the silent treatment for very specific situations, usually where there is no hope for the relationship. Here's a good rule of thumb: when reasonable boundaries have been clearly set and are violated more than two times, and consequences (like taking a *complete* break from the relationship) have been clearly and kindly stated each time, then it's appropriate and necessary to walk away for your own emotional health.

Chapter 10

Mindfulness, Mantras, and Gratitude

Time travel can be helpful when you do it as part of your self-led EMDR journey. But when it comes to working with on-the-spot anxiety, staying grounded in the present is key. Mindfulness exercises can keep you in the moment, whether through formal meditation or simple practices like mindful eating or walking. Even a few breaths to reset can make a big difference.

Mindfulness is pretty much what it sounds like. It's being attuned to the people, places and events happening around you. In chapter 7, you learned about the tendency to time travel in your mind and the problems that can arise if you have a hard time living in the present moment. Practicing mindfulness will help you be fully present and aware, so you can act and react appropriately to any given situation without getting overly anxious.

When you are aware and focused on the here and now, your autonomic nervous system is less likely to get triggered at inopportune times. When you exercise mindfulness regularly, you can develop the capacity to find your equilibrium a lot quicker after getting thrown off. It has the power to anchor you when life gets stormy. Each of us naturally possess this resilience skill to some degree, but strength training will ensure that you have access to your mindfulness "muscle" when you need it most. Here are tried, tested, and true techniques for practicing mindfulness in ways that nurture and cultivate it.

- Do the grounding and reorienting breathwork exercises you learned in chapter 8.

- Pause to reflect on and observe what is going on around you and inside of you.

- Choose from a variety of meditations that train your mind and body in awareness.

- Do yoga, pilates, tai chi, qigong, or another physical movement activity that requires you to be present and focused.

- Go for a nature walk and notice your surroundings using all your senses.

When I used to think about mindfulness and meditation, it would stress me out. During the practices, I would spend the whole time shaming myself about not having the right focus. But then I learned about a study best known as "the pink elephant experiment" (Wegner 1987). In the first part of the study, participants were told not to think about a white bear. As a result, participants could not stop thinking about the white bear. At some point, the white bear became the pink elephant—but the same results happened. Essentially, the study found that when you ask someone not to think of something, they will think only of that thing.

During meditation, we tend to try not to think about what's around us, get lost in time travel, or hop on emotional thought trains in order to be present. Rather than trying *not* to focus on these things (which the study shows is futile), meditation practice encourages us to notice what is going on inside. For us to successfully be in the present moment, we need to learn to get out of our heads and into our body. Even when we do meditations that encourage the use of our senses, our focus is on noticing the sensations that occur as we focus on what is there. So find techniques that help you drop your attention out of your head, down into your body. Then you will awaken to the moment.

Mantras Bring Calm Through Repetition

Scientifically, *mantras* can be defined as "prolonged repetitive verbal utterances" that have the power to induce a sense of relaxation and calm within the autonomic nervous system (Berkovich-Ohana et al.

2015). Studies found that the repetition of even a single word or sound showed significant shifts toward calmness in brain activity, even more than participants in the control group who rested without reciting mantras. Interestingly, the mantra-based utterances had soothing effects regardless of whether the words or sounds had particular meaning or not.

Some alternative practitioners rooted in Buddhist practices refer to mantras as "mind vehicles." Often the mantras they share are not even in the form of words we recognize or understand. They are specific syllables and vibrations, like "Om" or "So-Hum," that help people meditate and move beyond the thinking mind. This kind of work is helpful for some people, but doesn't necessarily resonate with everyone.

I refer to mantras as personally meaningful affirmations or phrases that you can repeat, and meditate on, as often as needed. They can calm your nervous system, help you shift a mindset or outlook, and aid your mindfulness practice. Mantras can be as simple as compassionate phrases or affirmations you tell yourself. Or they can be famous sayings that inspire you.

As you go through the following list of potential mantras, think about whether repeating each one would be helpful to you or not. Not all mantras, especially in the form of self-talk, are helpful to everyone—and some can even be triggering. Keep your own list of helpful sayings and reminders in your journal or binder, and refer to it as needed.

- You're having a rough time. You've made it through similar situations before. You can do this!

- You can move through this pain one breath at a time.

- You're doing your best with the tools you were given.

- My whole being—mind, body, and soul—has everything it needs to get through this.

- I can create my own path in life.

- I have the power to reach new heights.

- Slow and steady wins the race.

- I will remain positive, yet realistic.

- I will conquer my fears and become stronger each day!

- It's my choice what kind of day I will have. Nobody can take that away from me.

- I am curious and not afraid of being wrong.

- My body is my temple.

- I listen to my body and try to give it what it needs.

- I choose where to expend my energy.

- It's okay to ask for help when I need it.

Try to come up with some on your own. Say them either out loud or in your head, as many times as you need to. Write them down in your journal.

Shifting Toward an Attitude of Gratitude

Gratitude helps us refocus our energy toward the good things in our lives. It helps us appreciate how we're connected to others and the world around us. Acknowledging things we're thankful for shifts our attention from what's wrong to appreciating what's right. Here are some ideas for consistent times it might be helpful to slip gratitude meditations into your day.

Morning Thank-Yous: Some religions have a prayer that people say when they wake up first thing in the morning to thank their Higher Power for breathing life and new potential back into them for the day ahead. You can research this prayer in your own religion or come up with your own mantra. Mindfully say it as you awake each morning. You can also start the day by focusing on three things you're thankful for, in general. It can be big, like a loved one, or small—like a yummy breakfast.

Gratitude Rewind: Before bedtime, think back over your day and take an inventory of the positive things that happened. This gets your mind focused on positive thinking, plus meditation at bedtime is known to support better sleep.

Gratitude Sharesies: Once a week, spend some mindful moments thinking about the people you are grateful for in your life. Then plan gratitude-focused get-togethers to show appreciation. You can also make phone calls or send letters to express the gratitude that you've meditated on.

Navigating Life Equipped with EMDR Tools

Just like in video games, the journey to overcome anxiety isn't a straight path. It's more like an unpredictable treasure hunt, with a well-worn map, steep mountains to climb, sudden slides down, moments of pause, and unexpected turns. Sometimes we might feel like we're power boosting, with our growth feeling exciting and visible. At other times, it might seem like we've hit pause or even gone backwards, with our progress hidden behind the foggy clouds of challenges and setbacks.

These "setbacks" aren't blockades on our road, but necessary parts of our adventure. They're like wise old wizards, guiding us and offering unique opportunities to learn and grow. It's really important to be nice to ourselves when these times come, to remember we're just human, and that it's okay to trip, fall, and then get up stronger than before.

Every fall, every seeming wrong turn, every challenge we meet helps us better understand ourselves and our triggers, and witness how resilient we are. It helps us polish our strategies, tweak our responses, and ultimately build a more solid and resilient version of ourselves. These challenges aren't roadblocks. They're stepping stones on our path to becoming anxiety wizards.

The Sustainability of Growth

A big part of our journey together, maybe the keystone of our adventure, is the idea of sustainable growth. This quest to understand and manage anxiety isn't a one-time event or a temporary distraction. It's an ongoing journey, a lifelong process of learning, growing, and evolving.

The tactics you've found, the lightbulb moments you've had, and the practices you've learned aren't fleeting. They are timeless tools meant to be woven into the fabric of your everyday life, steadily guiding you on a continuous journey toward feeling better. The lessons from these pages aren't locked within the book cover. Instead, they're meant to be your trusty sidekicks, growing with you, reflecting your progress, and giving support when you need it.

As we wrap up this book journey, keep in mind that the practices you learned are most powerful when used in your everyday life. They serve as the guiding compass, the gentle nudge steering you toward wellness, even in the middle of life's wild storms. As you keep moving forward, remind yourself to revisit these lessons, keep chatting with your inner parts, and cultivate your growth in a sustainable way. Keep the momentum, knowledge, and lessons going. Welcome your future, powered by the past, rooted in the present, and hopeful for what's to come. The ending is just another beginning, and the path to wellness is an ongoing journey.

Setting Actionable Growth Goals

As you continue on, armed with newfound knowledge and a deeper understanding of yourself, it's important to turn this wisdom into actionable growth goals. The journey toward managing anxiety is truly about using that knowledge to spark real, meaningful change within yourself. An effective way of making this change is through SMART goals that are specific, measurable, attainable, relevant, and time-bound. These SMART goals will help you make a clear path toward growth, breaking down your bigger goals into bite-sized, achievable steps.

Goals should push your limits but not completely overwhelm you. The purpose of setting goals isn't to start a race against time or to set up an impossible challenge, but to draw a roadmap toward sustainable growth. It's okay if your first goals seem small or unimportant—every step forward, no matter how tiny, is progress. Over time, as your confidence and skills level up, you'll find yourself able to aim for and achieve even bigger objectives.

Continue to check back on these goals every now and then, assessing your progress, and tweaking as needed. Goals aren't static. They're dynamic, evolving creatures that should grow and change with you.

A Message of Hope and Encouragement

Our shared adventure through this book has been one of discovery, introspection, and growth. It has encouraged you to face fears, wrestle with anxieties, and find within yourself the strength and the tools to face them head-on. Through this exploration, one truth becomes super clear: within you, you have the power to manage your anxiety and to thrive.

As you move forward, carry this truth close to your heart. Let it be your lighthouse during challenging times, a reminder of your natural strength and resilience. No journey is without its battles, but remember, the journey itself is the reward. Every stumble is a chance to learn, every setback is an opportunity to grow stronger, and every victory is a testament to your strength.

Proceeding with Resilience, Together

The resources provided in this book and on the website http://www.integrativepsych.co/emdrforanxiety are always at your disposal, ready to lend support whenever you need it. The journey to manage anxiety isn't one you need to walk alone, and these tools and resources are your steadfast companions.

At the heart of this book, the essence of our shared journey, is hope and empowerment. We realize that we have the power within us to confront our anxieties, understand them, and control them, rather than letting them control us. We're not defined by our anxiety; rather, we're people of immense strength and resilience who happen to be managing anxiety. This journey, like every journey, has its challenges. But we're more than capable of meeting them. With the knowledge you've gained, the strategies you've learned, and the strength you've discovered within, you're ready to continue the journey toward managing anxiety, growing stronger and more resilient every day.

Acknowledgments

Thank you to all those walking the path of healing—those who have felt pain and still reach for joy. And to the therapists who meet others in their pain with courage and care—your work is sacred and deeply meaningful.

I am endlessly grateful to God for holding my hand in this process—and truly, in all of life. For the strength to keep showing up, and the grace that carries me through.

To my clients—thank you for your trust and bravery. You have been my greatest teachers.

To my colleagues and peers—especially those closest to me—thank you for the honest conversations and reflections that helped shape this work. To my mentors, who continue to guide me and remind me of what matters most—your wisdom and integrity light the way.

To the incredible therapists in my trauma training programs—thank you for showing up so fully. Your warmth, dedication, and community spirit inspire me every day.

To my in-person and online communities—thank you for your support, encouragement, and the thoughtful reflections that helped this work grow. And to those who follow my emails, LinkedIn, and beyond—your ideas and questions shaped this book more than you know.

To Jennifer Holder, my brilliant and thoughtful editor—thank you for your steady guidance. To Wendy and the team at New Harbinger—thank you for believing in this work. And to Rebecca Shapiro—thank you for helping me move this book forward when I felt stuck.

To my group practice team—thank you for letting me learn from you and grow alongside you. Our shared insights continue to deepen this work. And to the communities I've learned with—especially in IFS, EMDR, and Sensorimotor trainings—thank you for walking the healing path with such integrity.

To my parents—thank you for being my biggest cheerleaders and for your love and belief in me. Your willingness to grow with me has been a gift I carry everywhere.

To my siblings—Miriam, Chaya, Ruchie, and Mark—and their partners and children, thank you for being my rocks. Your steady love, humor, and unwavering support hold me up in more ways than you know. I'm so grateful to walk through life with you.

To my extended family and friends—thank you for showing up with practical help, playdates, and encouragement that created space for this book to be born.

And to my precious son—SY, your joy, love, and wonder are the heartbeat of everything I do. You are my why.

References

Anderson, F.G. 2021. *Transcending Trauma: Healing Complex PTSD with Internal Family Systems.* PESI Publishing.

APA PsycTests. Subjective Units of Distress Scale (SUDS).

Artigas, L., Jarero, I., Mauer, M., López Cano, T., Alcalá, N. September 2000. "EMDR and Traumatic Stress After Natural Disasters: Integrative Treatment Protocol and the Butterfly Hug." Presented at the EMDRIA Conference, Toronto, ON, Canada.

Beck, Judith S. 2011. *Cognitive Therapy for Challenging Problems: What to Do When the Basics Don't Work.* Guilford Press.

Berkovich-Ohana A., Wilf M., Kahana R., Arieli A., Malach R. 2015. "Repetitive Speech Elicits Widespread Deactivation in the Human Cortex: the "Mantra" Effect?" *Brain and Behavior* 5 (7).

Brown, F.H. 2006. *Reweaving the Family Tapestry: A Multigenerational Approach to Families.* W. W. Norton & Company.

Clift-Matthews, V. 2010. "Bonding Begins Before Birth." *British Journal of Midwifery* 18: 548–548.

Earley, J. 2009. *Self-Therapy: A Step-by-Step Guide to Creating Wholeness and Healing Your Inner Child Using IFS, A New, Cutting-Edge Psychotherapy.* Pattern System Books.

Erikson, E. 1980. *Identity and the Life Cycle.* W. W. Norton.

Fisher, J. 2017. *Healing the Fragmented Selves of Trauma Survivors: Overcoming Internal Self-Alienation.* Routledge.

Heller, L., LaPierre, A. 2012. *Healing Developmental Trauma: How Early Trauma Affects Self-Regulation, Self-Image, and the Capacity for Relationship.* North Atlantic Books.

Hendriksen, E. 2018. *How to Be Yourself: Quiet Your Inner Critic and Rise Above Social Anxiety.* St. Martin's Press

Jacobson, E. 1938. *Progressive Relaxation*. University of Chicago Press.

Ogden, P., Minton, K. Pain, C. 2006. *Trauma and the Body: A Sensorimotor Approach to Psychotherapy*. W. W. Norton & Company.

Peyton, S. 2017. *Your Resonant Self: Guided Meditations and Exercises to Engage Your Brain's Capacity for Healing*. W. W. Norton & Company.

Piedfort-Marin, O. 2018. *Journal of EMDR Practice and Research* 12 (3).

Porges, S. W. 2018. "Polyvagal Theory: A primer." *Clinical Applications of the Polyvagal Theory: The Emergence of Polyvagal-Informed Therapies*, 50, 69.

Schwartz, R. C. 1995. *Internal Family Systems Therapy*. Guilford Press.

Schwartz, R. C. 2021. *No Bad Parts: Healing Trauma and Restoring Wholeness with the Internal Family Systems Model*. Sounds True.

Shapiro, F. 1989. "Efficacy of the Eye Movement Desensitization Procedure in the Treatment of Traumatic Memories." *Journal of Traumatic Stress* 2: 199–223.

Shapiro, F. 1995; 2001. *Eye Movement Desensitization and Reprocessing: Basic Principles, Protocols, and Procedures*. Guilford Press.

Shapiro, F. 2013. *Getting Past Your Past: Take Control of Your Life with Self-Help Techniques from EMDR Therapy*. Rodale.

Siegel, D. J. 1999. *The Developing Mind: How Relationships and the Brain Interact to Shape Who We Are*. Guilford Press.

Siegel, D. J. 2010. *Mindsight: The New Science of Personal Transformation*. Bantam Books.

Tang, Y.Y., Hölzel, B., Posner, M. 2015. "The Neuroscience of Mindfulness Meditation." *Nature Reviews Neuroscience* 16: 213–225.

Van Der Kolk, B. A. 2015. *The Body Keeps the Score: Brain, Mind, and Body in the Healing of Trauma*. Penguin Books.

Weissman A. N., Beck A. T. 1978. "Development and Validation of the Dysfunctional Attitude Scale: A Preliminary Investigation." Paper presented at the meeting of the Association for the Advancement of Behavior Therapy. Chicago, IL.

Winnicott, D. W. 1991. *Playing and Reality*. Routledge.

Wolpe, J. 1969. *The Practice of Behavior Therapy*. Pergamon Press.

Esther Goldstein, LCSW, is a licensed clinical social worker, trauma specialist, and founder of the group practice Integrative Psychotherapy, where she and a team of therapists provide cutting-edge treatment to those seeking relief from anxiety, depression, and trauma symptoms. Esther also runs an online trauma training certificate program for therapists and educators around the world who are committed to deepening their knowledge, skills, and confidence in supporting those on their healing journey.

Esther has sprouted the community initiative, Integrative Community Care, where she and her group practice provide resources and mental health tools to surrounding communities. She is fiercely committed to raising awareness about health, and collaborating with leaders to give communities the support they need to keep thriving emotionally, mentally, spiritually, and physically.

Real change *is* possible

For more than fifty years, New Harbinger has published proven-effective self-help books and pioneering workbooks to help readers of all ages and backgrounds improve mental health and well-being, and achieve lasting personal growth. In addition, our spirituality books offer profound guidance for deepening awareness and cultivating healing, self-discovery, and fulfillment.

Founded by psychologist Matthew McKay and Patrick Fanning, New Harbinger is proud to be an independent, employee-owned company. Our books reflect our core values of integrity, innovation, commitment, sustainability, compassion, and trust. Written by leaders in the field and recommended by therapists worldwide, New Harbinger books are practical, accessible, and provide real tools for real change.

newharbingerpublications

MORE BOOKS from
NEW HARBINGER PUBLICATIONS

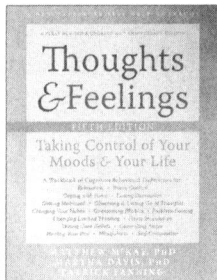

Did you know there are **free tools** you can download for this book?

Free tools are things like **worksheets, guided meditation exercises**, and **more** that will help you get the most out of your book.

You can download free tools for this book—whether you bought or borrowed it, in any format, from any source—from the New Harbinger website. All you need is a NewHarbinger.com account. Just use the URL provided in this book to view the free tools that are available for it. Then, click on the "download" button for the free tool you want, and follow the prompts that appear to log in to your NewHarbinger.com account and download the material.

You can also save the free tools for this book to your **Free Tools Library** so you can access them again anytime, just by logging in to your account! Just look for this button on the book's free tools page.

+ Save this to my free tools library

If you need help accessing or downloading free tools, visit **newharbinger.com/faq** or contact us at **customerservice@newharbinger.com**.